My Heart's First Steps

Writings That Celebrate the Gifts of Parenthood

JENNIFER GRAF GRONEBERG

Adams Media

Avon, Massachusetts

ᴄᴼ *For our children* ᴼᴼ

Published by
Adams Media, an F+W Publications Company
57 Littlefield Street, Avon MA 02322. U.S.A.
www.adamsmedia.com

ISBN: 1-58062-936-9

Printed in Canada.

J I H G F E D C B A

Library of Congress Cataloging-in-Publication Data
My heart's first steps / [compiled by] Jennifer Graf Groneberg.
p.   cm.
ISBN 1-58062-936-9
1. Parenthood. 2. Children. I. Groneberg, Jennifer Graf.
HQ755.8.H338 2003
306.874—dc21
2003001031

This publication is designed to provide accurate and authoritative information with regard to the
subject matter covered. It is sold with the understanding that the publisher is not engaged in ren-
dering legal, accounting, or other professional advice. If legal advice or other expert assistance is
required, the services of a competent professional person should be sought.
—From a *Declaration of Principles* jointly adopted by a Committee of the American Bar
Association and a Committee of Publishers and Associations

Many of the designations used by manufacturers and sellers to distinguish their products are
claimed as trademarks. Where those designations appear in this book and Adams Media was
aware of a trademark claim, the designations have been printed with initial capital letters.

Cover photograph © Francisco Cruz / Superstock

This book is available at quantity discounts for bulk purchases.
For information, call 1-800-872-5627.

"It is only with the heart that one can see rightly;
what is essential is invisible to the eye."

—*The Little Prince*
by Antoine de Saint-Exupery

Table of Contents

My Heart's First Steps / 65

Next Steps / 123

Reflections from the Wading Pool / 179

Introduction

Each night before bed, my son casually, nonchalantly, reaches out and grabs my ear, pinning me to his side. If he is particularly uneasy, he grabs both ears, pulling me close. I smell baby soap and milk, warm cotton and skin. Our breaths mingle, our heartbeats answer each other, and gently, he drifts to sleep. I am his, and he knows it.

It wasn't always this way. I was a nervous new mother. I'd read all the books and knew all the ages and stages, but none of it helped me. I was terrified. Too scared to let myself love this small, feeble being, all hunger and need. Helpless. One thing that new life had shown me was that living was an unpredictable and sometimes dangerous thing. That a baby could flourish under the care of my husband and I suddenly seemed to require a great leap of faith, and I wasn't sure that we were up to the challenge, after all.

I was frantic for the confidence that only experience brings. Surely, I'd overlooked the books on parenting written by mothers and fathers, everyday people like myself. Where were they in my towering stacks? But I'd missed nothing. They weren't there. So I proposed to make one where there had been none, a notion that is nothing new to parents, who already know that from a small, quiet wish, tremendous things can develop.

With my husband Tom's help, we created a flier requesting first-person accounts, essays, or poetry. We included guidelines and submission information, and at the bottom of the page, we added, *Help spread the word. Tell others about this project.* I handed fliers to parents with children, sent them to roommates from college, posted them in libraries and doctors' offices. I bought a small classified ad in a parenting magazine and put another notice in a writer's magazine. Parks, play groups, any place with children was fair game, until there was nothing more to do but wait. I registered for the smallest mailbox at the post office, reasoning that when I turned the key, I'd barely notice the tiny, vacant slot.

But the writing came. Envelopes appeared, large and small, thick and thin, from across the United States, Mexico, Italy, Israel. Five hundred fliers disappeared and I photocopied more and, later, more still. Friends told friends, neighbors went door-to-door, libraries and colleges and writing programs displayed the submission information. In our rural town of four thousand people, the sudden influx of mail must have been noticed, but the postal employees were too polite to ask, until I whispered to one, "Writing by mothers and fathers about being parents."

"Ah," she answered, curious. "Can anyone write something?" and I knew I'd found a compatriot.

Suddenly, happily, I had piles of reading. I was awed by the many beautiful stories written in scraps of time and stolen moments in the middle of the night. From them, *My Heart's First Steps* was born, a collection of nearly one hundred selections from mothers and fathers across the country, during various points in their parenting journey. As people, we have differing opinions on politics, religion. We are new parents; we are grandparents. Despite our diversity, there is much that we share.

We worry. We grapple with pregnancy later in life, or with infertility. And after our babies are born and we are past the many uncertainties of conception and development, our anxiety continues. We whisper our fears to each other any time we're in groups, *Not sleeping yet,* or *Still on a bottle. Only eats Goldfish crackers,* we confess. *Hasn't walked yet. Not talking.* When you have kids, we find, there is always a wolf at the door. We try to ignore it. But as our offspring grow, so do our fears. We are afraid for them in the world that we all must share.

We struggle. Our feelings about parenthood are complex and sometimes contradictory. There are moments when we are aware that no other work is as important as raising children. Other times, we bemoan the drudgery of it, the endless cleaning, the mountains of laundry, the work. We learn humility. Our bodies betray us, our emotions overwhelm us. But we forge on, hopeful and brave, teetering between the perfect parents we expect ourselves to be and the people we actually are, despite our best efforts at self-improvement.

We watch. We witness with joy our children's first smiles. We share first steps, first words. Later come the first fishing trips and paper routes. Our babies grow up. Our children become parents and we become grandparents.

We dream. We remember our former selves and the ease with

which we moved through the world without a diaper bag. We imagine life without little ones, magically suspending the duties of parenthood to become the carefree couple at the table for two by the window, if only momentarily. And all the while we try to prepare ourselves for life after our children have grown, which is the hardest thing of all to picture.

Our team colors are pink and blue, the colors of parenthood. Pink baby buttocks, chubby fingertips, rosebud lips. And the sweeping colors of the dawn, which so many of us are present for each early morning. The troubled sleep of our children wakes us to the blue shine of the moon, and it is in the blue glow of a nursery nightlight or by the flickering blue light of a television that we soothe our children back to sleep.

We rock. At all hours, in chairs or on foot, back and forth. Back and forth. It is a rocking beat, one that every parent learns. One-two. One-two. It is the pink rhythm of life, a sound deeper than blue. It is a heartbeat.

It's been four years and parenthood has become a part of me, as essential as air. I am nourished by my role as a mother and I am marked by it as well. I am part of a wobbly, wonderful clan of people, all mommies or daddies, who are also changed by the experience. We wear sturdy shoes, wash-and-wear clothes. We can sleep standing up; we can sing "I'm a Little Teapot" with a straight face. We are agile, ready for peekaboo or Catch Me or Ponyback at a moment's notice. We are magic. We can turn flour into play dough, snow into ice cream. Our kisses heal. We hold the future in our arms, several times a day. And there is a light in our eyes. We know the sweetness of it, the crazy joy, the pure love you find when you give your heart to a child.

My Heart's First Steps is a community project, pulled together from our collective parenting experiences. It would not exist without the contributors, who shared the stories closest to their hearts. I can think of no greater generosity; there is no better gift. It is in this spirit that I offer *My Heart's First Steps* to parents everywhere, new parents especially.

—Jennifer Graf Groneberg
Polson, Montana

Beginnings

Naming the Baby

∾ JOYCE M. FISCHER ∾

Kate

⑨ When the test shows a clear, dark, unmistakably pink line, I still have trouble believing it. Yes, we planned and timed and even sent positive mental energy, but we are talking about a miracle here. I feel a slight pulling in my pelvis and I want to grab the bakery lady by the wrist and say, "I'm going to have a baby!"

Then the first, dark cloud. What will we name her? (I simply know it's a girl like I know my hands are attached to my arms.) My mouth goes cold. I have to create the most integral fact of this child, the first word she will walk into a room with or be judged by, even before she shows her true eyes, her sturdy body.

Kate. She will be Kate. Sensible, practical, strong, capable, a friendly, open face. I try calling her Kate, and it is only after a few days that I realize Kate would be a great next-door neighbor, but I am carrying a miracle between my hips, and there's just no way she is a Kate.

Willow

Small, quiet waves of metallic nausea follow my every move, but I am enchanted. Here is my chance for redeeming grace. To create a person of such quiet, calm beauty that my own bitten fingernails and short-waisted body are lifted into an easy, graceful peace. Tall and slender, with a long neck and upturned palms, eyes the silver-green of leaves in afternoon shade. The name drifts from the lips like the gentlest of breezes. Then I see the cruel trick that the name would be, if she were short and round and full of a snappy strength that gives her voice a rich shine. I can't carry a Willow in my body.

Ginevra

Echoes of a rich, Italian past. Regal, intelligent, clear in speech and manner. Dark hair with a complicated face and tiny white teeth. In Italian, *Ginevra* means "juniper." I'm pleased when I picture dark green needles with clumps of dusty-blue berries like the new shape of my belly, hard and round. I keep Ginevra, until one night I dream of a strong girl with straw-colored hair who plays field hockey and begs for a mountain bike. She shortens her name, as soon as she can, to Ginny.

India

I lay naked on the chaise longue for hours, watching the stiff mound of me, my breasts flowing to either side like lava on an old volcano, the squirming inside me both familiar and mysterious. I spend afternoons reading novels. India: exotic, complicated, mysterious, darkly beautiful. I see exquisite fabrics, intricate sari silks with hot reds and blues and shimmers of gold, or the beautifully flowered cottons of the ball gowns India Wilkes wore in *Gone With the Wind*. I see my child, India, in breathtaking fabrics, lace socks, and fine leather shoes, cherished.

"The problem is India Fischer," my husband says. "Why?" I ask, as if I don't understand what he means, but I do. India Fischer could be a muddy, saffron color in a J. Crew catalog. Short-sleeved cotton sweaters in Evening Pearl, Merlot, Provence Slate, Portuguese Sage, and India Fischer.

Julia

My husband proposes Julia. I like the music of it, the pinkish golden light that shines behind it. He rubs my belly and holds my hand when he says it. Julia. We try Julia for a few weeks, until a sourness creeps in, as if I ate a cookie right before bed and then woke with the sugar gone sour and thick in my mouth. I hear the sweetness in Julia, but I don't trust it. My husband is angry for a while, but I learn something very important. No one stays really, truly mad at a pregnant woman.

Zoe

Queasy pain wakes me, my body starts to empty, and I taste panic. We tried on names like bargain shoes, discarded them for good reasons or none, and now I don't know who is coming out of my body. I shake with the pain. I want to remember what life was like before, to go backward just for five minutes. But I can only open to her.

The midwife holds the mirror and I can see her. She pauses, eyes closed, her face a statue suspended for one last moment. Her head turns and then her shoulders, and her whole body is out, alive, eyes open and bright, eyebrows lifted, surprised and amused. The answer, in the end, is as uncomplicated as her body on mine, her lips on my breast, her clear face. From the Ancient Greek, the name is simple and pure, the meaning even more so. Zoe. Life. 🖤

Womb Music

KAREN HOWLAND

This August when I birth you, I will
be next to the breast of the earth
burrowing ten toes into sun warm soil
sinking into grass as you ascend

dark clean and healing   *a clearing*

nature embracing nature
mammal and plant and angel
nourishing with enduring rhythm
blood and sap and spirit beating

dark clean and healing   *a clearing*

mysterious and still, we listen
to the cottonwood, communicating
with the east wind, sun and moon turning
around my belly, gentle revolutions

dark clean and healing   *a clearing*

the crickets and I rub our response
leg-serious, pulling songs from secret places
a whole green chorus whispering skin
skies of muscle, cell, and bone music

dark clean and healing   *a clearing*

my body is one red breath burning
beneath the sky until you arrive to suck
red and blue stars into your alveoli
we will be many, we already are. 🖤

Welcome to the World, Baby Girl

∽ JENNIFER GRAF GRONEBERG ∾

The call came in the early dark of three A.M. "We're having a baby," Phyllis said, with a happy breathlessness. Phyllis is my friend and Sonja's friend, and we were both honored with invitations to the birth of Sonja and Jeff's fourth child.

I remember driving through a tunnel of tall Douglas firs, following the white light shining from the headlights of my car. I left behind my son, Carter (*"Mommeeee"*), and my husband, Tom, in our warm bed, snuggled together in a king-sized down comforter. I cried as I drove, partly for myself, for the birth of our son that I remembered as if it were yesterday, although it had been two years ago already, but mostly overcome with what I was about to witness. Driving in the predawn hush past all the sleeping houses in town, their early spring lawns greening under the automatic sprinklers that seemed to sputter to life just as I went by. Sonja and Jeff's house was high on a hill, and the town below that we all called home was still; even the streetlights paused their blinking yellow, yellow, yellow. The snow-topped mountains to the east glowed in white starlight, everything in perfect, bright anticipation.

Five cars were parked in front of the house and even from the street, I could hear the low moaning. As I approached the front door, the keening rose, "OhmyGodohmyGod," to a trilling, then a ululating cry. I opened the front door, which was unlocked, and took off my shoes and coat, then went up the stairs.

Phyllis was waiting for me. "No talking, no touching," she whispered. These were the ground rules.

"How long have you been here?" I asked.

"Since midnight," she said. "I came at the first contractions, but there wasn't much to do, so I waited to call you. I asked Sonja how I could help and she said, 'Clean the bathrooms.' So it's been three hours. I think we're close." She nodded at the video camera in the corner, which I didn't remember how to use. It was my ostensible reason for being there, although I am technologically impaired. When Sonja asked if I would videotape the birth, I didn't have the heart to tell her that I couldn't even work my microwave. I'd arrived at her house a few weeks earlier for a training session, during which I was hopelessly distracted by her endearing smile and her three beautiful children. We spent the afternoon talking about almost everything except how to work the video camera. She and her husband were new to the community, recent transplants from Seattle. When I asked her why they'd moved here, she explained that in her old neighborhood, every yard was fenced, and every fenced yard was almost always empty. The kids were in child-care programs all day while the parents worked. She said they'd wanted a neighborhood where their kids could run. "That's what we have here," she said, "kids running in and out all day." As she spoke, she put her thumbs up and scissored them back and forth—front door, back door, revolving. I liked her right away.

And now that it was time for the baby to come, I wished we'd talked more about how to use the video camera. I sat outside the open doorway of the bedroom, camera on my lap at the ready. On the bed was a woman who I assumed was the midwife—short salt-and-pepper hair, slim, fit; wearing small glasses, a tan, ankle-length cotton skirt, and a striped knit shirt. She was bare-footed. Her eyes crinkled shut when she smiled her kindly smile, which was often. There was an assistant, a young, olive-skinned woman also dressed in an ankle-length cotton skirt, hers plum, and a forest green, long-sleeved shirt. She was also bare-footed, her toenails painted metallic purple. They whispered about toenails painted to match their stetho-scopes, murmured about vitamin B for circulation. As they spoke, I learned that the younger woman was an apprentice.

There was a royal blue birthing tub in the corner, which reminded me of a larger version of the inflatable pools everyone sets up for children in the summers, but this was larger and sturdier and all about work—the work of bringing a baby into the world. The older woman periodically checked the thermometer in the tub to make sure it read 100 degrees. There was an oxygen tank with a face mask in the corner. Surgical gloves spilled across the top of the ordinary wood dresser. The handle of a black plastic bag was looped over the doorknob. There were hand-held scanners that beeped and mea-sured. Fresh flannel sheets, white with multicolored flowers, covered the bed and the duvet. There was a wooden rocking chair in the corner and a baby crib next to the bed.

This was a newly painted room in a newly remodeled house. The faint smell of fresh paint lingered in the stairwell, and white paint spattered the tips of the clogs in the cubby hole by the front door, Sonja's. There were remnants of the other children, ages two through six, who were staying with a friend—mismatched pairs of small tennis shoes in the cubbies, a giant bottle of bubbles on the top shelf, a tiny stool in front of the bathroom sink.

And in the middle of it all were Jeff and Sonja—she, sitting on the edge of a chair, and he, kneeling before her, holding her hands in his; the strong features of her face, the curve of her bare white shoulders, the full moon of her tummy, all backlit by the single, slim torchiere in the corner. They held hands together like this, her face wracked with pain from the contractions, his low murmuring, then the peace, the relaxing of her face, the two of them aglow, luminous together, hands clasped tightly, holding together, shining together as if in prayer, the two of them engaged in a prayer as old as the earth.

I had the camera then and was clumsily trying to convey all of this, when Sonja says, "It's coming." She slides into the warm water of the tub, still holding on to Jeff, and it is happening. The midwives, for whom I suddenly feel a great fondness, move into place. The moment is here, the four of us form a circle around Jeff and Sonja, and then something is not right. The baby is out. She is blue. There is a cord around her neck, thick and white, wrapped too many times. I back away, put down the camera, lose track of things. "Please baby, please baby, breathe," Sonja is saying. Phyllis and I move away to give the midwives room. They are working, pulling Sonja out of the water and onto the bed. The oxygen tank in the corner suddenly becomes vital. Phyllis comes to me and we hug, holding the embrace three beats too long. She has lost a baby and knows what the pain is like. I have lost nothing—all I know is the birth of our son, strong and howling into the fluorescence of the hospital delivery room. It instantly occurs to me, as abruptly as if I'd been sucker punched, how vulnerable we all are. How much we all loved this baby, had already loved her before she was even born, and how much we needed her to be born safely and surely, to this beautiful and strong mother, to this brave and funny father, to this family of remarkable and hearty children. In this moment, I understood clearly the meaning of mercy, all of us begging for it in our private and desperate ways.

The baby is breathing. She is alive. We are okay. For now, for this moment, we are fine, filled with breath and love and life. Phyllis leaves, to go home to her husband and four boys, ages two to fifteen. Jeff dozes, his head on Sonja's shoulder, his hand over the head of their new baby, who nurses at Sonja's breast. I ask Sonja what she needs. "An apple," she says. I go downstairs into the kitchen and from the drawer, I remove a black-handled paring knife. On a cutting board near the sink, I slice an apple into small, bite-sized chunks. The kitchen window overlooks the town, still asleep, which overlooks the lake, skimmed with mist. On the sill there are two smooth stones and three small, Easter Egg tulips in an empty glass jar. I twist the tap and add an inch of water. Outside, a cat jumps onto the windowsill, crying to come in, and as I look out again, I realize that dawn has come. It is spreading over the world, all the colors of the night mixing with all the colors of the day, and it occurs to me that everything, this morning, is shades of pink and blue.

Upstairs, I deliver the apple to the sleepy threesome, and inquire what the midwife team might need. The younger one asks me to crush some ice and put it in surgical gloves for Sonja for later, when she might "be experiencing discomfort upon urination." I do, smashing the ice in a plastic bag on the cutting board with a heavy pan. The cat is gone, the sky now more pink than blue. The rubber gloves are unwieldy and their fingers pop out at me comically as I try to fill them. I am so happy and everything seems silly. I put two ice-filled gloves, now in the shape of hands, into the freezer, which is overstuffed with casseroles, frozen Tupperwares, and a half-gallon of Tillamook Peanut Butter Fudge ice cream.

I deliver some of the ice chips upstairs. The air is warm and moist and smells like blood and body fluids, slightly metallic and bleachy. I pull open the white sheets that cover the windows and wipe away the condensation, so that Sonja and Jeff and the baby can see the light breaking over the mountains and across the lake. It seems impossible that any other day could be as good as this day and I want them to see it all unfold. There is talk of breakfast and coffee and I volunteer to find it. The roads are empty, the sun is up. The lawn sprinklers are off. Here and there lilac bushes have started to bud. The only place to go is the bakery, and they're "not really" open yet, I'm told by a busy middle-aged woman with shoulder-length dark hair, but she unlocks the door and lets me inside anyway. I explain to the woman, and to the two old men in feed store caps drinking coffee at a table in the corner, that a baby had just been born.

"Look at her," the woman says of me, stopping her work. "She can barely talk." She is right. I manage to order four coffees, and she adds huckleberry scones, banana-bran muffins.

"What's the name?" they all want to know, and I can't answer. I don't know. In all of the rush, in all of the anticipation, through all of the fear, I never thought to ask. What might you call it? What could you say? It was only later that I knew the word I should have said to them.

"Grace," I would have answered. "Lucia Grace."

All along that's what it was, and I'd been blessed to witness it. 🌿

El Producto

PETER KROK

How I shared him bud his skull
into the new born air

—a son blossoming
in my welcome hands

—a root now
of my blood . . .

And I lit an El Producto
in the Nova going home. ❦

Not According to Plan

∾ SUSAN EVANS ∾

I'd done my homework: read *Parenting Without Tears,* bought educational toys, researched the Upper East Side pediatricians and signed on with Dr. David Smith, the baby doctor's baby doctor. I was so adept at Lamaze breathing I could pant my way through a filling and never flinch. Even so, my firstborn caught me off guard.

She was late, not a day or two, which I could attribute to faulty math, but by more than a month. Just as I was resigning myself to being pregnant forever, my obstetrician declared the placenta was disintegrating, and with more enthusiasm than I felt the situation warranted, sent me straight to the hospital to induce labor. I soon discovered the reason for his glee. In 1970, New York Hospital had just acquired a fetal heart monitor to track babies' heartbeats during strong contractions, and I was to be his test case. My husband, George, and I felt ridiculous, with our puny bag of wet washcloths and Lamaze lollipops, up against the gleaming monitor and the tsunami of staff that came with it. We had envisioned a serene, deeply meaningful birth, the kind where mother and child bond instantly and beautifully to strains of the *Moonlight Sonata.* This was to be more like giving birth on the Ford assembly line.

None of my research applied to the intense labor pitocin induces. Instead of the gradual buildup I'd read about, I found myself having pelvis-wrenching contractions at fast-paced, ninety-second intervals. I puffed and panted gamely, and attempted a plucky smile for the entourage of doctors who streamed through to see the new technology in action. After six hours, though, my spirits were flagging, and I had barely begun to dilate. My team of experts decided to let me rest overnight and get an early start in the morning.

"You'll probably continue to dilate now that you've started," a perky nurse assured me. "It won't take any time tomorrow."

I looked for this angel of mercy the next morning as the professional army reassembled at my feet, but she was nowhere in sight. I was in sore need of some of her professional cheer. Labor was intense but ineffectual, and the only person who seemed concerned was me. Finally, around 9 P.M., an intern stole a glance at me, instead of the monitor, and realized I looked a "bit wan." Within minutes the baby was delivered by forceps.

To no one's surprise, it was a girl. I'm the first daughter of a first daughter of an only daughter. Girls in the Whelton line are our stock in trade. The surprise was her appearance. A perceptive nurse assured me her dark body hair was "not uncommon" in overdue babies and would probably "shed" in a matter of days. I'd been given a lot of false hope the past two days, though, and "shed" seemed like an ominous verb. I was relieved to no longer be pregnant, but not at all sure this baby could possibly belong to me.

"What's her name?" she asked.

"Courtney Carkhuff Robinson," I told her, including our last name in case they'd forgotten it in all the excitement.

According to the birth certificate, Courtney was twenty-two inches long and weighed seven and a half pounds, with the requisite number of fingers and toes. I don't recall any mention in the delivery room of what a beautiful baby she was, but by the time George and I got on the phone to the grandparents, she was gorgeous.

The next morning I woke up with a stinging nether region and what appeared to be a half-full bag of laundry on my stomach. I was in a room facing the East River with the sun streaming in. Either the room was on fire or I was. I couldn't tell where I started and the sun ended. I was high on new motherhood.

At seven A.M. Courts was wheeled in by a bedraggled night nurse with a "quittin' time" look on her face and a bottle. I was New Age enough to attempt natural childbirth, but in 1970 I thought hippies were the only ones who breast fed. Our first few hours together were as unexpected as the birth had been. Courtney viewed the bottle with suspicion and me with hostility. By the time the morning nurse came in, we were both in tears, and I was frantically searching for the exit. For the first time in years, I wanted *my* mommy.

Three days later, the nursing staff had calmed us both and initiated an uneasy mother/daughter truce. Courtney was eating, I'd quit wailing, and there were isolated moments when we beamed adoringly into each other's eyes. I was informed that Courtney's beatific grin probably indicated gas, but whatever the reason, I was charmed. We were sent home with much assurance that everything would "be fine," but I knew better. Nothing so far had gone according to plan, and I suspected nothing ever would again. ❧

Bringing In

LYSA JAMES

After the first contractions,
a time when everything
shifts, you become
more than the sum of two parts.
You begin to travel beyond your body.
The shifting
of blood and bone.
Beginning with faith

you dive down, breathing in
a musky scent.
Shafts of pale white float
in the dim light
unlike the body in the days
before birth when the belly shudders
with the tremors of the almost born.

Further down you go,
a long struggle. The steady return
of breath after breath
until sight dims in the silty depths.
Only breath, and the pulsing womb
amongst the dwellers of the deep
whose wings keep the rhythms steady.

Your breath is dense, weighted
by pain. You drift between
volcanic ache and not remembering
the spirits who push
with you the whole of this birth down

to the grounding place. The sound
of heartbeats
what you breathe, what you
are becoming.

Faster your breath,
and harder until pale
blue and silver,
like the underbellies
of fish, this baby arrives
in a thunder of heartbeats.
The force that moves child
into life, into blood—
this aching world. 💜

Birth Choice

∾ NORMAN WASSERMAN ∾

Someone in the room said afterward, "Brooklyn folk bring their own frontiers with them." The room was in Eugene, Oregon, 3,000 miles away. There were nine people in that small room and the shared feeling was indescribable. For each of us it was a glorious moment of life. Especially for me.

But it didn't come easily.

My "willful" daughter, Jennifer, born and raised in Brooklyn— P.S. 8, Packer, Stuyvesant—had announced long distance that she was pregnant. A year before, she had moved west to marry an Oregonian and settle in Eugene, a city with strains similar to Brooklyn—freethinking, liberal, hospitable, skeptical. She informed us quite casually that she was going to give birth at home with the help of a pair of midwives. At twenty-five, it was her first pregnancy. The sonogram showed fraternal twin fetuses, automatically regarded as high risk by medical professionals.

I am myself a native of Brooklyn, and like most pre–baby boomers, tend to cling to some of the tried-and-true ways. My bias in favor of science leapt to the fore; secretly, I viewed midwifery as a throwback to the Dark Ages. My wife and I practiced the Lamaze method with the births of our two children, but the deliveries took place in a hospital under the direction of a trusted obstetrician.

I pointed out to my daughter—who is a vegetarian, a conservationist, an earth creature of basic values—that idealism has little to do with the birthing process. No home setting could match the facilities, equipment, atmospheric controls, hygiene, and staff of a hospital maternity ward or birthing center. Suppose there was a need for incubators or other life support? I advised her to get the best ob-gyn in town to work in conjunction with a midwife if that's what she wanted. The bottom line, I argued, has to be the safe, healthy delivery and immediate aftercare of mother and infants: "Give the newcomers to the family the best birth day you possibly can," I thought.

Jen is a Cornell graduate, and while I was pontificating she was exploring every option as if she were a lab researcher. She honed in on one doctor who seemed to be okay until he suggested a chemically induced delivery two weeks before term (mainly to accommodate his vacation schedule). He also prescribed medication that was contraindicated for pregnancy in the *Physician's Desk Reference.*

Another doctor was part of a nine-physician practice and essentially a "roulette wheel" would determine who would attend her delivery. She visited hospitals and birthing centers and was turned off by the sterile environments and restrictions on the participation of midwives. She read books, interviewed pregnant women and midwives, and attended classes and a conference where she volunteered herself as a subject for hands-on study. At one point she was negotiating to import a midwife from Portland who was an acknowledged "twins maven."

When I persisted with sensible arguments into her eighth month, Jen accused me of being a negative factor and injecting fear into a positive, uplifting experience. No way would she deliver in a hospital attached to three monitors and strapped down in the archaic stirrup position (in use since King Henry VIII decided he wanted a birds-eye view of his wives and mistresses giving birth). She cited chapter, verse, and statistics about obstetricians who perform needless episiotomies and C-sections. (Did she suspect one twin would be a breech baby?)

The issue was closed: She was working with three midwives, and it would all happen at home. And would I please keep my redundant, conservative, New York, overly paternal advice to myself? We had a long talk on the phone afterward and came to a tentative peace.

My wife and I took a late flight from New York and after a two-hour drive from Portland, arrived in Eugene at four-thirty A.M. All of the lights in the house were on. One of Jen's water sacs had broken but contractions were weak and irregular. It was clear it was not going to be an easy labor. We were shunted off to our B&B a few blocks away. When we returned that afternoon, Jen was not there. To induce stronger contractions, one of the midwives had taken her on a three-hour walk—an unorthodox procedure but one that proved to be productive.

The first twin was born breech. It took several hours during which Jen labored mainly in a semisquat position and on her side. We arrived thirty minutes after the birth following a sleepless night waiting for news. Jen had cut the umbilical cord herself. She smiled wearily at us, nursing one of the twins with pleasure. The thought occurred to me that in a hospital my daughter would now be heavily sedated with a Cesarean incision across her middle. The baby, six and a half pounds with red hair, was perfect. He whimpered every few seconds, in a barely audible singsong. One of the midwives explained that this was not extraordinary; he was signaling the other fetus.

Exhausted, Jen had to gather her strength for the second birth. We waited outside, holding the firstborn. After nearly five hours we were summoned in. A dark crown was visible, and then the entire head appeared; the face turned blue and white in rapid succession. Then came a mighty contraction-and-push, and the father's sure, loving hands caught the little body—virtually the same size as his brother. I was told that I watched with a classic mouth-agape expression.

Am I a convert to midwifery? Yes. I met three of the most caring, knowledgeable, experienced, and sensitive women that I could ever hope to meet in any profession. In aggregate they have assisted mothers in the delivery of some 650 babies, including my two grandsons. The midwife route is not for everyone, and I am sure midwives would be the first to agree. But mainly I am a convert to my daughter—her sense of self, her strength, conviction, and frontier freedom. These days I'm more likely to keep my wide-open mouth shut. 🌿

Paternal Punctuation

∽ JOHN REPP ∽

The morning we discovered my wife was pregnant, I wrote a poem in which I addressed our future child as "my eentsy comma." I had just taken my first shower as a prospective father, some of the water swirling down the drain tears of awe, dread, relief, giddiness. I hadn't expected to feel giddy when the "+" appeared in the tiny window of the pregnancy test, but I did, and out of that surprise came the poem. The meandering sentence I had written for forty-seven years had ended with a loud exclamation point, and now a barely there bundle of cells had begun to write a new sentence more thrilling and terrifying than any I could compose myself.

Right from the start, our complicated comma did the comma's job well: It separated items in a list ("We need a crib bumper, four dozen diapers, booties, all-in-ones, hats, sleep sacks, and a case of beer for the father."), it helped join together independent clauses ("I want to give the kid what it needs, and I want to sleep and not work overtime."), and it marked off initial phrases or clauses ("In a perfect world, she would walk, talk, and exercise bowel and bladder control at birth."). Yet, like any comma securely employed, it retained flexibility, even disappeared for long stretches during which Kathy and I spoke and thought about matters far removed from our looming parenthood. Not for us a claustrophobic, obsessive monitoring of "the baby."

Oh, we read our share of books, saw our share of intrauterine photographs, watched several videos that made painfully vivid the matter-of-factness of the miracle of life. It seemed no secret of fetal development had gone unrecorded. We marveled at how these amazing events went on regardless of how we felt or what we did. I remembered watching time-lapse film—perhaps in a high school health class or on a *National Geographic* special in the gray days before cable—starring an impregnated human egg that morphs into a zygote resembling a minuscule, parasitic mark of punctuation scrawled on the wall of the uterus. Time passes. The zygote becomes a fetus, a pudgy semicolon bobbing in its own private, nutritious pond. At last, assuming good genetics and good luck, an entirely new, entirely whole human being head-butts through the pelvic door. Only now this wasn't just any impregnated egg or "a" zygote or "the" uterus. This was Kathy's uterus and "our" genetic package we first called "it" or "the kid," but which soon became "he" or "she" as our creature's existence became more and more undeniable.

Despite all the evidence, though, I never during Kathy's forty weeks of pregnancy imagined our actual child, what his or her face or hair or limbs would look like, what he or she would sound like cooing or screaming. In some fundamental way I didn't believe our child existed until the crown of his head filled my palm on the morning he entered our world.

A month old now, Dylan has long since convinced me he was inevitable. In fact, he insists on it every minute. What he demands, he gets, providing we translate his garbled verbs right. He's in a Prince Imperative Mood: "Feed me!" "Hold me this way!" "No, that way!" "Change me!" "Let me cry, for God's sake!" When he feels generous, he sleeps or coos or gazes raptly at my shirt or his mother's necklace. He furrows his brow like Beethoven. He fans his fingers like Vincent Price. After particularly strenuous bouts of crying, he resembles Sid Vicious singing "My Way." He has excellent taste in music: Ben Webster, Lucinda Williams, and Mozart calm all but the most mysterious bouts of hysteria. The other night, he paid close attention when Derek Jeter came to bat, but next season I'll exercise my fatherly influence and point him toward Nomar Garciaparra.

So far, fatherhood has been confusion, shopping, sleep deprivation, anger, and housework punctuated by short stretches of bliss. Sometimes I realize how lucky I am. I keep reading and hearing what being a father means, how I will feel one way or another as I become more experienced and Dylan more articulate in expressing his pleasure and pain. I've begun to think the truth may be more simple and less comforting. My son will teach me fatherhood. Period. 🌢

Partners

CHARLES GROSEL

We're partners now,
you and me,
partners every day.
Partners in milk,
in bottles and nipples,
sour hanging on our clothes like tinsel,
and don't forget the diapers.

Used to be,
fathers didn't have
this poop and pee love,
this squeeze the head through the collar,
pop the arms in the sleeves,
catch the froggy feet
and snap like the devil love,
this please go to sleep,
don't you want to sleep?
be a good boy for Daddy love,
this cooing, crooning, blue-eyed,
drunk from a good feeding love.

Curl into that question mark,
grunt like you're birthing yourself,
blast it out either end.
Ah, there's the smile. Ain't this the life?
Get it down fast, Daddy, 'cause
in no time at all we do it again. 🍂

How My Children Came to Me

∾ DENNIS DONOGHUE ∾

In the middle of the night I sit up in bed, strain my ears, then nudge my wife. "Was that Beatrice or Apphia? Maybe it was Justina?"

She listens, doesn't hear anything, curls away from me, back to sleep. I get up anyway, move stiff-legged through the cool air to Justina's room. Her bare feet poke through the ribs of her crib. I grope the mattress for her socks, roll them over her feet, straighten her out, and arrange the blankets. In the other bedroom, Apphia lies on the covers in her crib, her bottom in the air, one sock off, her breath coming in whispers. I turn her on her back and tug her to the head of the mattress, then move across the room to Beatrice, who's wedged against her bed railing. I roll her onto her back. Pale moonlight washes over her face. I watch her sleep and wonder what the sound was, or maybe I just imagined it.

I'm forty-five years old and have three daughters under three years of age, all of whom came to me under quirky circumstances, which makes me think that they chose me, or were chosen for me, perhaps by the same source that produced the sound I did or did not hear that got me out of bed to check on them.

My Heart's First Steps

For two years before the three arrived, my wife and I tried to have a child. A miscarriage, testing, drugs—Carla and I in the upstairs bathroom, me with a syringe full of Profasi aimed at her hip, Carla clutching the sink while her sister and mother waited in the kitchen for us to go out for pizza. After one round of insemination, we were notified that the clinic would close for a month of bookkeeping. In seven weeks we could try again. Frustrated and defeated, we stopped the treatments.

Not long after our decision, we attended a general meeting at an adoption agency. Fourteen months later, we sat with Beatrice's biological mother in a hotel room in Guatemala City. She held Beatrice and kissed both her cheeks. After handing our eight-month-old back to Carla, she rubbed the tears from her own cheeks. I'd become a father at last, after the lengthy and unsettling process of adopting another man's child.

A month later Carla told me she was pregnant. I sat on our bed, hands shaking, blood draining from my face, not believing what I was hearing.

"We had sex one time since we got back from Guatemala," I said.

"I know," she said incredulously, staring at the home pregnancy kit she held in her hand, at the nuances of color that told our future.

In January, after thirty-four hours of labor, Apphia was born. I ran my fingers through Carla's soaked hair, massaged her scalp as the baby crowned. My wife was in agony and I had the worst headache of my life. A nurse weighed Apphia in a basket under a bright light, then jabbed a needle into her thigh with such nonchalance that it made me sick to hear my daughter cry in pain for the first time.

For months, Apphia nursed in what seemed like ten-minute

intervals. Beatrice was up, too, wanting her mother. I was exhausted, teaching sixth-graders all day and running up and down stairs most of the night. I slept in spurts, and went through my days at school forgetting where I'd put things and what I'd said to people. After lunch, when the kids were doing seat work, I'd nod off, then catch myself dreaming about a full night's sleep.

The agency informed us in May that Beatrice's natural mother was pregnant again, and when we said yes, I wondered if we were crazy. With a toddler not yet two and a five-month-old, another adoption was a risk, and perhaps we were ignoring reality for some sort of higher ground that would later bury us. We restarted the paperwork, got fingerprinted a second time, and spent the last of our savings. When we traveled to Guatemala City to collect Justina in February, my sciatica was so bad I lay groaning in a fetal position on the linoleum floor of our hotel each morning of our five-day stay. Perhaps my body understood something I didn't.

Now, fourth months later, I can stretch my daughters on the floor to change their messy diapers. I bind the diapers up as tightly as baseballs and think how when this stage is over, I'll save a fortune. But the extra money won't make up for the fact that there'll be less touching and holding, less silly talk and eye contact. Someday, it will not be a good idea for me to give them baths like I do now, or creep into their rooms in the middle of the night to check on them. They'll want their privacy more than they'll want their father.

That's fine, I tell myself at the supper table when they're screaming and refusing to eat and Carla has had it—they've been like this all day, she says—and the beer I opened an hour ago is going flat. With baked macaroni on my lap, sippy cups on the floor, and two hours to go before bedtime, the mystery of my children isn't so magical. It takes all my strength not to scream back at them, not to get up and leave the room. Lack of an escape hatch consumes my thoughts, the two hours before bedtime an impossible length of time to get through. But by eight they'll be scrubbed and ready for bed, followed twenty minutes later by my wife and me, another day behind us.

I don't sleep as soundly as I did before I was a father. I wake up more often and can't go back to sleep as easily. Now, after I've checked the kids, I lie listening, waiting to hear something again.

"She'll go back," Carla assures me, touching my shoulder. "Just give her a minute."

I think about how each of my children came into my life. Uncertainty gave way to possibility, which in turn became opportunity. Once, twice, three times in less than two years, as much as by chance as by plan I became a father, my children like cards dealt from a deck into my hand. Out of necessity I changed from a person who went to bed each night and didn't stir until morning, into someone who listens for night sounds, who walks lightly on his feet to aid and comfort, and for this, my children deserve all the credit. 🐝

Love and Sleep

✺ MALAINA NEUMANN ✺

✺ I will tell you about my daughter, Isis, whom I dreamed of when she lived in the womb. I dreamed she was quiet and mystical and I believed these dreams to be prophetic. I was a live wire as an infant, but I felt my child would be serene and spend long hours staring into my face or playing with her toes, giggling. I will tell you about her newborn days, which are not so far behind us that I can romanticize them. My child cried, she howled, she stayed awake twenty hours and slept four, the opposite of what the books described. She cried in her crib and in my arms and in the car and in the grocery store. I felt like the whole world was looking at me, wondering how I could be so inadequate. She hated to ride in the car or in the sling. Tricks I'd used with other people's babies proved useless on her. Sometimes I'd look at her and think that she just was not happy about landing on this planet. Maybe somehow she'd been tricked.

This is not a story about simple solutions. It is a story about personalities and who we are before we can even speak. It's 9:55 and she is up for the third time since we put her to bed. I get frustrated in the night; sometimes I get angry. I miss the old days when my time was my own and I could unwind in the evenings; watch a movie from beginning to end. People tell me I am glowing but I feel subhuman.

I want to tell you about Isis. I want to tell you some of the things I know about her because I have never loved anyone the way I love her. No one has ever opened my heart the way that she has. The love I have for her makes romantic love look puny. She inspires me to be good and try harder. She has the dreamy blue eyes of my husband and a devilish gleam I try not to claim. When I look at the photos of her newborn face, I am teary. She looks so helpless and new.

As she grew, her disposition improved. Crawling helped; walking made things even better. She spends her day exploring and wants to spend her nights the same way. The object of my undying affection has soured my sleep for forty-four weeks straight. And I treasure sleep.

Isis was the girl in my belly, then my bones shifted in labor and she moved through me. She was a little red snail without her shell and she cried. I knew that I loved her, but I did not know what that meant. But tonight as she sleeps in her all-too-brief shift, I know that I love her more than desire. My heart is now large enough to hold her inside.

Yesterday she licked me on the jaw. She brought a rubber duckie to my breast to nurse. She made the little piggy sound for the first time and laughed. She played peekaboo from behind a pair of boxer shorts, my own blonde-headed sprite in a T-shirt and diaper, absolute perfection. I can tell you tonight that I love my child more than summertime; I love her more than the wind. I love my child even more than sleep. ♥

Masculinity Meets His Daughter

TODD W. PALMER

My macho days are over now.
Hard to believe
That rough and tumble self is really dead.
So many times before,
Like a stubborn brush fire,
My wild-eyed side burned through
Those wet, maternal blankets
Thrown by women meaning well.

Good-bye to my hard-driving, deep-sleeping dog,
Who caroused with the boys
And only played with manly toys,
The tempestuous, two-fisted me,
Who ran himself ragged time and again,
And muscled his way to the top of the heap,
To the jagged-edge cliff of self-reflection
Where he'd wrestle himself
And win,
Then stand tall, proud, and alone, looking down,
Laughing at life's little obstacles,
Tough as a he-man can be.

Strange how, not with a bang
But a whimper in that gentle,
Terrible, first good night
As a father bolt upright in bed
At the sound of my daughter's cry,
The macho me wandered away.

I now sing a rusty lullaby
To will her back to sleep.
But when her fever soars,
My blood runs cold with fear.
At night her coughing
Takes my breath away
Until she takes her next.
When she can't tell me where it hurts,
I feel the ache bone deep.

But awakened somewhere inside me
A maternal voice whispers,
This too will pass, my son.
Still, my heart stops cold
At a bump in the night,
I perceive the house settling
As a serious threat,
And I look down on my daughter,
So fragile in the dark of night,
And marvel at the weight of change she brings.

My macho days are over now,
But I am the man of the house.

New Mother Song

ROBIN BRADFORD

I miss my old brown sleep,
dreams that used to show me
a picture of myself.
Now I wake and my strange breasts
beneath each hand
feel like bellies of sleeping puppies.
I miss things I've never done:
singing in a choir, painting by the lake,
running a marathon, shopping
at outlet malls. I mourn
my silent cup of coffee.
I don't miss reading much till suddenly
it clobbers me
and I cry for the Sunday magazine.

I lost my necklace in the rush.
Open, open, open, the midwife said
while my husband sang a song from India.
By dawn the pink roses he'd brought opened
just like they do in India.
A night, a day passed
and then a thought: this pain is something
I will hold in my arms.

In Africa, I'd read, a mother makes a figure of herself
        from river clay
and wears it from her neck until the birth.
Then she breaks it on the rocks and it falls back into
        the silt and waves.
I arrange the towel, the tub, the bottles
and test the water.
Dipping in your pink curled feet,
I let go of the fragile thing I was. 🌿

With Child

∾ JENNIFER GRAF GRONEBERG ∾

There is a tiny cluster of islands west of Japan where mothers are treated as newborns for the first month of new motherhood. Ordinarily, the women work very hard each day, making camellia oil or harvesting shiitake mushrooms or repairing fishing nets. Yet after childbirth, a mother is wrapped in blankets with her baby and is expected to do nothing more than nurse and recuperate. Other women care for her, speaking baby talk to her in small, high voices. They help her regress, so that she can recover.

As a new mother overwhelmed with fatigue and emotion, I thought of this place, which I first read about in T. Berry Brazelton's *Touchpoints,* often. I was drawn to the idea of it because as I imagined them, these customs honored the work of bringing a child into the world. They nurtured the one who pulled life from the darkness, carried it to term, and delivered it into the light. A woman needs time to catch her breath after such work. I did not know it then, but after the birth of my son, what I needed was to allow myself the time to be a newborn mother.

This is what happened: Nights of endless nursing. Worry. Exhaustion. In the darkness, I wrapped myself and our baby in a patchwork quilt, laid on the floor, cold with winter, utterly spent, and fell asleep in the blue glow of the nursery nightlight. I awoke near daybreak, terrified. I hadn't put the baby back in the crib. Had I smothered him in my sleep? But there we both were, warm and safe, my son breathing softly, his perfectly pink mouth a rosebud in the dawn. It was the first time in weeks that I'd slept long enough to dream.

Then there is my husband. We had been married six years before the birth of our son when suddenly, we were no longer two, but three—a new father, a mother-baby combo, a newborn family, shakily trying to find our way. We wondered at what we'd done, marveled at our new roles as parents as strongly as we feared them and the million small changes they brought to our lives each new day.

And somewhere in the midst of it all, the diapers and the spit up, the cooing and the tiniest of smiles, the tears and the laughter, we did find our way, just as every mother and father do. What I learned is this: It's not about having all the answers; no one does. It's the work we do, the time we spend, the love we show in our attempts to try to find the solutions. It's in the way my husband learned to hold our baby close to his chest and twirl, twirl, twirl the night away. It's listening to polkas over and over again, because it's the only thing that soothes our child. It's learning to listen to your heart when it tells you to love deeply. The love you give never leaves you. When you think it's gone, close your eyes and remember. It's all there. Yours again, to give again. ❧

For a New Mother

ANNE McCRADY

On good days you will wake first,
the others still inside
their own rounded dreams.
New day on your skin,
you will rest against the surface
of an eggshell of solitude
you have grown to need,
to find only at dawn.

Moving in shadows,
you will shiver in the coolness
of a day not yet broken loose.
Slipping on softness,
pulling hair into loops,
rinsing regret from your face,
you will savor the vacuum,
the shy optimism of a day
just beginning to understand
its possibilities.

Later, life will become full
of . . . well, life!
The sun's toothy grin
will widen into gregarious noise.
Conversation will come in tumbles.
There will be questions
with no quick answers.
Love will splash its way around.
That will be later.

But, first,
early, so early that
light tiptoes around,
everything will be easy,
weightless.

You will hush even the urge
to call someone to watch with you
the blood-rush of sunrise,
the heart-throb of morning.
This will not be to share.
You must take it.
It is what you need,
first. ❧

Beginnings

Sleeping with the Baby

CHARLES GROSEL

oh, the grief we get
for sleeping with the baby:
news clips from Grandma,
comments all around—
You'll smother him . . . .
It isn't natural . . .
What about sex . . . ?

if only they could see him
hooded in the sheets like a tiny monk,
hands outstretched to each of us,
protected in the circle
of our bent legs touching at the knee,
our hands meeting above his head
like Michelangelo's *Creation*

if only they could smell his butterfly
breath, sweet as whipped cream,
could hear the hummingbird heart
thrumming beneath inhalations
and exhalations full and free at last,
could feel the tingle of fingers
on skin instead of Plexiglas

if only they could behold his face asleep,
trace the curve of perfection
along his cheeks, his eyes quivering
beneath rosy lids laced in blue filigree,
lashes full, thick, and long, curving
like the turned up brim of a baseball cap,
lips muttering in prayer or benediction

if only they could wake with him
to morning light, turtle head
popping up to the sun, eyes shining
as he flops about like a porpoise,
matching the jays shriek for shriek,
scatting his morning song. 🐦

One Month, Two Children

∾ SARAH WERTHAN BUTTENWIESER ∾

It's a few hours before I leave for the hospital to give birth to our second child. My husband, Hosie, our toddler, Ezekiel, and I are standing in the driveway. I hold Ezekiel close for an extra hug. In the photographs, I look ripe. My belly is stretched large beneath the purple-and-rust African-print sundress I borrowed for two pregnancies. Ezekiel is propped over my bump. My face is round and fatigued, but I am smiling. Ezekiel is smiling, too, at the silliness of trying to place his hat upon my head. I'd just made his lunch, dressed, and fed him breakfast. I tried, in my mind, to drink him in, knowing that the next time I'd see him, I'd have another baby.

Ezekiel is a beautiful almost-three-year-old. He has uncut fair, fine, and slightly curly hair. His wide, green eyes are shaded by lush lashes. I tried to memorize his broad, coy smile and his full cheeks as emotional fuel. I wanted to forge in my memory what it felt like when holding him was the norm, and he was not yet measured in comparison to anyone else. Those photographs, while not so beautiful, capture this moment at the cusp of change. The first month of having two children has been, for me, marked by ambivalence: great joy but profound sorrow, fatigue but exhilaration, confidence alongside confusion.

My Heart's First Steps

Awaiting a second baby's arrival, I worried about my inability to give enough to my firstborn. Dreams of losing Ezekiel plagued my pregnancy. In one, I was arrested and about to be taken to prison, where I'd be able to see him just fifty days out of the year. The night sky was pitch-black, the air cold and damp. Police cruisers were parked, lights flashing. My father, inexplicably on the scene, said with alarming indifference, "Don't worry. Ezekiel will have Hosic and his grandparents, and you'll have fifty days a year to visit." Desolate, I cried out, "I don't want to be his mother for fifty days a year! I need to be his mother every day." I was absolutely helpless. Meanwhile, my belly ballooned and my lap disappeared, just like in the picture books we'd read to prepare older siblings for the big event. Ezekiel grew increasingly clingy. I felt clingy, too, but also exhausted. I needed rest. He would demand "Mom-my" in a particularly pained tone for things like being tucked into bed, in what was the beginning of a push and pull between closeness and a new form of separation. Already, the baby had wedged itself between us.

The baby, when he arrived, was warm, purplish, and slippery. He cried out with insistence and unfathomable newness: "Rah, rah, rah . . ." Lucien, with his velveteen skin, was a pure, limp bundle of softness and need. His fingers were delicate and infinitesimal. His toes were even smaller, pooled like thick, round drops at the ends of his squat feet. He gleamed. Slick black hair capped his head, and his body seemed malleable enough to fold back inside me. I couldn't believe how tiny he was. Ezekiel walked into the hospital room wearing a dazed expression. He seemed huge. Old, too, as if all traces of babyness had slipped away in the playground. He looked awed; he looked sad. My heart broke.

Soon after Lucien was born, I would walk into Ezekiel's room in the morning to get him out of his crib. His first word of the day was "Mama." I'd silently muse, *I am so in love with you.* Lucien didn't hold a candle to that love. So what if he hadn't yet had two years and eight months to find such a big place in my heart? Ezekiel, in a sleepy voice, said slowly, "Huggy." And we'd stand, him on the changing table, me in front of him, and hug for a long time.

Those first days, when I was homebound and couldn't go to the playground, or take Ezekiel to school, or to the Y for his Saturday-morning gym class, were interminable. But sitting was too uncomfortable for me to drive the car. I had to nurse the baby. I had to rest. While I wanted to be with Ezekiel, my energy level had dropped to a shockingly low level, and I couldn't keep up with him. From my distant corner upstairs in the bedroom, I could hear him singing and stampeding. The wild toddler had slipped beyond my grasp. I managed to appear downstairs while he was strapped into the high chair, so I could talk to him while he ate. Later, I snuggled with him in my bed, reading stories to him before he went to sleep.

Physically, the first week was as if I'd been hit by a train. I could not sit, so I lay down or stood up. My bottom felt horrible: aching, burning, tender, sore. There were stitches where I tore. The astringent scent of witch hazel and alcohol, soaked on pads or poured into warm sitz baths, permeated the room. I was nursing constantly. From an initial drop that concerned the visiting nurse, Lucien's weight began to climb. At a week, he had regained his birth weight plus a

☜   *My Heart's First Steps*

few extra ounces. A week later, he'd added another pound. From there, he kept going. His thunder thighs have folds, his cheeks shimmy, his belly hangs over his diaper.

But when I glanced toward my bloated, marshmallow-soft stomach, I felt demoralized. I carried a stretched-out mass of excess smack in the center of my body. No longer pregnant, I wanted to look like I was no longer pregnant. I desperately needed a haircut. People said I looked radiant. I didn't feel radiant, although I was smitten with the sturdy little creature I cradled in my arms. It's odd to feel so completely crappy and yet blissful at the same time. Ecstatically miserable. Awfully happy.

Then, there is sleep. Four A.M. and we've had not more than two hours of uninterrupted slumber, and that's a generous estimation. I'm so exhausted I can't really remember exactly what I'm supposed to do. Nurse. Light is just beginning to seep into our bedroom, a dusty gray that is more shadow than light and seems to hold the last hope of night with it. I pray for more sleep. I would give anything for it. This is the moment I consider sending the little creature back. His entire body engages in sucking. He snorts, snuffles, hoots, and wriggles as he ingests. He is so soft and so sweet. Although I'd love him that much more if he slept for two whole hours after this, so I could wake to a sun-dappled full morning. Sleep is like a gauge: when full, the day begins in a sprightly manner and everything that you require—energy, patience, an even temper—is possible. When empty, you can write the day off. It's a terrible, horrible, no good, very bad day, and your fondest wish is to move to Australia. Alone.

While I can't quite remember what I felt in the first month for Ezekiel, I do recall it was more intense; I was landing on Planet Parenthood. Now, I'm simply moving to another area on the planet. Lucien is a plump little baby with spiky, dark hair, at least so far. Perhaps he has my eyes. He has huge cheeks and a rosy, dark complexion that will handle sun easily, sure to turn nut-brown each summer. People constantly say what a pretty baby he is; his face quickly snapped out of newborn mushiness. To snuggle close to Lucien, to nurse him, to oogle, google, change a diaper, give him a bath, all these things are pleasurable. He smells like a baby, that fresh, untainted scent. He makes a lot of noise when he nurses, little squeaks and squawks. Sometimes, he says, "Ung-gee."

I have to get to know Lucien in short snatches. A month in, although he doesn't yet feel familiar, or even part of the family, I can't imagine life without him. In comparison to the love I feel for his big brother, my feelings for Lucien resemble an absorbing, exciting crush that might develop into something real. Ezekiel barges into the nonverbal cocoon I weave around myself and the new baby to insist on endless medleys from *The Wizard of Oz*. He wants apple juice, not grape. He has questions like, "What is that called, the thing that attaches the banister to the wall?" He calls Lucien "the little baby," or "babe-o," or "the little guy," "Leoleoko," and "Luciento." His kisses verge on overzealous puppy licks. And as if by some magnetic pull, his hands gravitate to Lucien's face, which he wishes to explore and to smush.

So, I'm in two places. More accurately, I'm splitting myself between two places: the busy world of the precocious two-going-on-three-year-old, and the juicy newborn's primal state. I am called upon to have reason and patience, then to have stamina and patience. I must keep Ezekiel on track with naptime and bedtime, meals to eat, books to read. I try to remember which breast Lucien last suckled, so I can start there next. Parenting still includes everything we do with Ezekiel, but the baby concerns have resurfaced. We've returned all the way back to burping. Meanwhile, I crave a reminder of myself. With manic determination, I clean my closets, tossing away entire eras of my life: sheer flowered skirts, tailored jackets with severe shoulder pads, little black dresses. Grasping at strands, I start to exercise slowly. I write in my journal.

I'm amazed at how well Hosie and I are navigating the choppier waters of this new, complex burst of activity in our lives. When I can cultivate the necessary patience and mindfulness, I revel in the relative simplicity of my task: I am being called upon to love these three people with my whole being. Most of the time I also experience a very strange emotion—contentedness. The challenge for me is to find balance in a dynamic state, because there is less order in a house filled with two children than in a childless one. As a parent, too, I'm setting myself on a new course, by resolving to grow my heart in such a way that I love larger, but make each baby less precious, less fragile, less personal. I see this happening with my little Lucien. I trust his crying more than I did Ezekiel's. I trust my ability to care for him. I trust in his happiness, too. And I trust in mine. 🌿

After Two Months of Nursing at Night

Liza Hyatt

You were born with August's tomatoes
but now it's already October,
the last warm days and nights of Indian summer,
and as we sit in the dark
with the windows open
and crickets chirping
amid dry leaf rustle,
I draw you to my breast
and your lips and tongue
tug at my nipple
and milk gushes into your gulping coo,
each coo humming into my breast
like you're playing a kazoo,
singing straight into my heart.

Breastmilk, I have been told,
changes taste with each day's meal,
sometimes sweet with oats and brown sugar,
or fishy and sour with lemon-sauced salmon,
so tonight's would be
garlicky and green with this summer's pesto.

I remember summers on the farm—
home to three generations before
we had to sell—
how raw milk from the guernseys tasted like grass
and everything was discovery,
the first sounds, sights, and tastes
of what living sounds, looks, and tastes like,
always wonderful, always surprising,
like a calf's suck on my finger with its soft, thick
    tongue,
like drinking a meadow in one glass of fresh milk,
like being swallowed up each day by a world so new
I could taste grass growing in it.

Everyone asks me:
Has she slept through the night yet?
And my husband has announced for days:
It's going to rain and turn cold by the end of the week.
I say·
What's the hurry?
Too soon there will be winter and nights of unbroken
    sleep.
The autumn rains hold themselves back
and I enjoy waking, feeding you,
floating together in the dark,
you sucking basil-tinged milk,
me savoring you, the savor teaching me
that I hold the most precious moments of my life

as I hold you to my breast,
and the flavor of this moment
is so ripe, so rare, so sweet,
I taste joy growing in it
and so night after night
as long as I can
I will do just this.
Rock you and nurse you
and savor you and for brief moments
almost believe
that I am finding the way
(and love is the key)
to make time stand still. 🌸

Secrets

M. S. TUPPER

I discovered my secrets late in life.
They had been with me all along,
disguised as blood that dribbled out of me once a month.
Surely Health Class covered this, you say;
you're a grown woman.
And somewhere in the back of my brain I'm sure I did
have a clue, all those years.
Somehow I had just enough presence of mind
to keep my secrets safe.
But the truth is I never really understood
what this was all about until one of them
was tempted outward with a seed—
I kissed her infant cheeks and held her tight.
Now instead of gazing in the mirror at my face,
I stare first at the bundle in my arms,
then at my abdomen below.
What else lies inside?
Constantly I dream of doing it again.

Constantly I am tempted to draw out that stream
of colorful scarves like a magician,
wrap it around my belly,
wear it at my hips.
Time is passing.
It is so, so hard to stop. ♥

Second Son

∾ MARCIA GERHARDT ∾

I hear the smallest cry from the cradle in the next room and creep silently from my bed. Reaching for my son, I scoop him close then back myself into the seat of the rocker. As I loosen the buttons on my nightgown, my breasts tingle, grow taught, and begin to seep.

I hold him against me. Soft as down, his hair is thinning at the top. A coarser circle of dark hair surrounds the base of his skull. He resembles a tiny monk. I hum slowly as I rock, imagining the future with my second son. The house is still. Unfamiliar peace permeates the air. I am in awe of this child I thought I'd never have. We are perfect. Everything I've ever wanted to be, I am at this moment. There are no regrets, there is nothing to change.

He loosens his hold. I breathe his warm baby-smell. Tiny eyelids struggle as his mouth blows milk bubbles that pop against his lips, slick as seal skin. I bring him to my shoulder where his head flops heavy in the hollow of my neck and I can feel the rhythm of his breathing. I suck in my breath, tuck the quilted blanket close, and rock a little faster, humming a made-up tune as if my very life depended on the staying of this moment. ❧

How It Happens

∽ CANDY SHUE ∾

You find yourself standing in front of the stove, stirring a pot of boiling water filled with bottles and caps and nipples and pacifiers and soft-bite spoons. You are still wearing your pajamas, even though it is late in the morning, a time when "respectable" men and women (as your father would say) are dressed in suits, sitting in offices, making the world go round.

You, however, are bleary-eyed from lack of sleep, your back aching from walking endless circles around the house with Baby while singing "Onward Christian Soldiers." You have no idea why, but it is the only song that seems to soothe her deep in the night. And although you have begun to hate the song yourself, these days you don't question anything that works.

Everybody told you about the back thing, so you are not surprised. What does surprise you is how much the rest of your body hurts. Your wrists are so sore that you have to use both hands to lift the pot of water to the stove. As a kid, you used to make fun of your mother because she always asked you to open jars of peanut butter, pickles, and maraschino cherries. Now all that teenage karma is coming back to you, just like she said it would. Rubbing your swollen elbow and feeling like you've suddenly turned into your mother, you think, "So. This is how it happens."

At five months, Baby (Light of Your Life, Bundle of Joy) is not sleeping through the night, so neither are you. Each afternoon, when Baby finally takes her nap, you have to decide what to do: sleep, eat, exercise, take a shower, go to the bathroom, write letters, pay bills, wash the dishes, or do the laundry. Sleep usually wins. You love sleep, you crave sleep. Sleep has become your drug of choice and dreams are your television.

You long to read a book, but can only manage snatches of inconsequential magazine articles sandwiched into the cycle of feedings and changings and washings. For a while you tried to read books, but your mind kept racing ahead, thinking about all the things you needed to do. Feed Baby in half an hour, oh, but first you should put a load of clothes in the washer, and later you have to go grocery shopping, but where is the list you started? And after you read the same page for the tenth time, you gave up all hope that you would ever finish a novel again.

Your hair is askew and you can feel a troublesome cowlick popping up like the proverbial weasel. Baby loves this rhyme. Her face breaks into a crinkly-eyed smile and she chirps with delight each time you recite it, which you do again and again (even though it makes you feel foolish) because you just can't get enough of her drooling, toothless smile.

You eat what you can when you can, because if you wait until you get to the grocery store you will starve to death. If Baby is napping, you furtively wolf down a sandwich and chips, afraid that the sound of your chewing will wake her. Otherwise, you eat haphazardly with one hand, balancing Baby on your hip and hoping that your bad example won't turn her into a tiny junk food addict. Your weight, which had initially dropped after Baby was born, is creeping back into the pregnancy range.

Your exercise regimen, which used to include step aerobics and mountain biking with your husband (The New Progressive Father), has been reduced to walking to the park or the grocery store or your mother/baby playgroup. It makes you feel pathetically insular, but you also thank God that you don't live in a neighborhood where you'd have to drive everywhere, because the thought of getting Baby in and out of the car several times a day makes you break out in a cold sweat. The world has shrunk to the size of your house, so you keep the radio on all day just to hear other adult voices. You glean little bits of news and make a mental note of items to sprinkle into your conversation, so people won't think you have gone soft in the brain.

Your wardrobe has changed, too. No more snappy suits or dresses that require dry cleaning. When all of your clothes smell like sour milk, investment dressing is not an option you can consider. You look wistfully at the silk shirts and suede skirts in your closet as you reach for your black wash-and-wear leggings and oversized denim shirt. Baby delights in pulling your earrings and necklaces, as if any shiny, dangling object exists purely for her delight. For you, jewelry has become an instrument of torture, instead of a fashion accessory.

Your old friends from the office always start conversations with the same question: "What are you doing with all your free time now?"

When you answer, "What free time?" they smile and agree, "Oh, yeah, being a mom is definitely a full-time job."

They also say, "You must be getting strong, carrying the baby around all day."

A vaudeville joke leaps to your mind. "Sure," you reply. "And someday I'll be able to pick up a cow."

Ba-da-boom.

But you worry that what they are saying to one another is, "She really has let herself go, hasn't she?"

Even your husband, The New Progressive Father, might think this, although he would never say it out loud. He changes diapers with the best of the NPFs, but his life goes on much the way it always has with work, projects around the house, tennis with his pals. He doesn't panic (Who will take care of Baby?) when his boss sends him out of town for a meeting. He doesn't have to make special arrangements just to get his hair cut. You, on the other hand, are always there. Always available. Always on call, like a doctor trapped in a bad horror movie, "Night of the Living Dead Interns."

Your husband is as loving as ever, though you are too exhausted to appreciate it. The two of you steal whatever moments you can together. Baby fussing in the middle of the night becomes a chance to discuss the pros and cons of various types of birth control, although with things the way they are, it's mostly a moot point.

"Don't worry," he says, as the two of you drift off to sleep spooned together like children. "It's only a matter of time. You'll be back to normal soon. I read all about postpartum blues in a magazine. . . ."

And you think drowsily, "No, you don't understand. This is 'normal' now." You have tried to tell him, but he seems to think that your pregnancy was a temporary condition, like an extended case of the flu.

"Pregnancy is temporary," you tell him. "Motherhood is forever."

"Parenthood," he corrects you, jokingly. "Motherhood and

Fatherhood make Parenthood." But it's not a joke, you think now as he lies beside you, snoring ever so lightly. You had never noticed that he snored before. You had never been awake to hear it.

The life of working from nine to five (or later), of having drinks with your coworkers, of not thinking about anything except the next project, belongs to someone else now. You knew that this would happen, because you helped hire and train your replacement, The Bright Young Thing who had just returned from living in Paris for a year. You knew it would happen, but it is still a shock to see how easily life at the office goes on without you.

Your old friends tell you everything that's happening at work, in a misguided attempt to keep you plugged in to the real world. And, as you listen to their stories about which client came in for a meeting and which big contract didn't get signed, you think, "What was I doing there, if I wasn't irreplaceable?" It makes you feel better in an awful sort of way, but in your darker moments, you imagine The Bright Young Thing sitting at your desk, running the meetings you used to run, exuding the perfect amount of sexy professionalism that you used to, as if it were the latest perfume from Saks Fifth Avenue.

Now the only thing you exude, if the benevolent smiles of strangers are anything to go by, is Perpetual Motherliness. It's as if now that you've fulfilled your biological purpose, you've become everyone's mother, even to the guys who used to flirt with you shamelessly at the local record store.

On the other hand, you've watched The New Progressive Father bask in the light of much female attention whenever he plays with Baby at the park, and it prompts you to wonder if all those generations of the hunters versus the gatherers have indeed had a genetic effect on human gender traits, just like they told you it had in your high school science class. "Oh, no," you think, horrified by the many clichés that could turn out to be true over Baby's lifetime.

Before Baby was born, it seemed as if you never had enough time, because you were always working. Now, it seems as if you have plenty of time to think about all the things you want to do, but no time in which to do them.

When you stumble into the nursery for the two A.M. feeding, and you see the beatific smile on Baby's face as she nuzzles your breast, you think about what a paradox it is: how this child has taken away your life, and how she has also given your life back to you. You can't explain it because you're not even sure how it happened, but your life began again when your child was born.

How do you explain that everything you do for Baby—feeding her, bathing her, changing her, even getting her dressed for the third time in the same day—has become a ceremony, a ritual of giving? How do you describe the feeling of well-being that envelopes you in your rocking chair, with Baby dozing on your lap and the dog sleeping in the corner? Your moments of happiness are so small and sublime that words are too big and too clumsy to capture them. The gift your daughter has given you is the time and space to recognize these moments, so tiny that they slipped by unseen, day after day, every other day of your life.

How can you explain this to anyone? You wouldn't have believed it either, if you were living your old life of meetings, deadlines, and conference calls. You wouldn't have believed it at all, except that it happened to you. "So," you think, holding Baby close and breathing in her deep, warm, velvety smell, "this is how it happens." ❦

My Heart's First Steps

Introductions

∽ PETE FROMM ∽

"You'll be thirty-seven before he's a year," my father marvels, missing few chances to remind me. "Your little brother [the last of his six children] was already two years old by the time I was your age!" True enough. There's no arguing with the calendar. Nolan, our only child, is seven months old now. By the time he's my age, I'll be seventy-four. Seventy-four or nothing.

So, wise and wizened, Rose and I have tried to take this whole baby thing in stride. We've tried not to go crazy pushing Nolan into anything. We didn't take him wilderness rafting when he was three months old, didn't take Rose out elk hunting when she was eight months' pregnant; none of that macho stuff you hear about out here in Montana that always makes you wonder what they could've been thinking.

Instead we've tried to let him show us what he's ready for. And what he's shown us from the first is that he loves watching anything that moves. A ceiling fan holds him riveted. Leaves, branches of them shivering in the wind, mesmerize him. A walk through the bright lights of the grocery store, shelf after towering shelf of colorful displays, causes him to gape in amazement. He's never once cried in a moving stroller.

But still, a stroller only goes so far. And it only goes there on reasonably flat ground. Once he could hold his head steady, we introduced him to the backpack. Same effect. As long as I keep walking, the sidewalk can fascinate him.

The only other thing he loves as much as motion is water. Tub time's nothing but shrieks of excitement, frantic pumping of arms and legs, wide-eyed stares at the wonder of splashing. Fascinated by motion, by water. Safe in the backpack. Perhaps he was telling us something.

So, while the sun crested the mountains last week, I got Nolan fed and changed, wrapping him in clothes to keep the sun from touching his skin. As I strapped him into his carseat and pulled his baseball cap tight around his head, he grinned up at me. Something was up.

Yet he only made it about ten miles before falling asleep. He cried as he went down, hating to miss anything, and afterward I drove too fast, trying to get the rest of the trip over with while he was out. Nolan slept till we hit the gravel. Then he woke quietly, as he does sometimes, staring up at the clouds, harmless billows of cumulus broken by huge gaps of late summer blue.

As I wrestled him into the pack, Nolan kept up his watch, twisting to look every time the wind rustled the leaves of the giant cottonwood we'd parked under. I looked, too, having almost forgotten the silvery underside of those leaves, the dark green tops; the way wind flashing through skittered the shadows, turning two colors into a whole sky-full.

While I searched through my fly box, Nolan reached for the flies, more new mysteries for him. I pulled the hooks away from his fingers, deciding to go with what I had on, a grasshopper. A hot, windy day in August, why not?

I was still trying to discover a way over the barbed wire enclosing the old bridge, when Nolan first saw the water. He sat up straight in the pack, his knees leaving the small of my back. As I stepped over the wire, pushing it down with my hands and stretching over the rusted barbs, Nolan fell forward, then to the side. He grunted with the effort of keeping his head upright, fighting not to lose sight of this amazing thing he'd discovered—a whole world of shifting light and sound; a river of water stretching farther than any seven-month-old mind could imagine.

My first step into that water, shallow and cold, made Nolan squirm. He wanted to get down there and do the splashing himself, I figured, but when I let him try, he cried at the cold. Back in the pack he started to squirm again, too excited by all that motion to sit still. I walked him along until he grew quiet, rapt.

The fishing was slow, nothing rising until some tiny white mayflies began to hatch. Switching flies, I managed to land a few dinky rainbows, nothing over six inches, but, turning so Nolan could watch, I kept saying, "There's the fish, Nolan, there's the fish!" every time they'd jump, shaking at the hook.

Before letting them go I held each fish over my shoulder, toward Nolan. He reached slowly, carefully, as he does toward any-thing unfamiliar. I expected his hand to recoil at the slippery cold touch, but, instead, he held his fingers on the fish's flank. He didn't shriek or jump, just held his hand against the side of the fish, serious.

By the time I gave him the whitefish, he'd apparently made up his mind. He wrapped both his fists around it and pulled it toward his mouth, which gaped open, one-toothed, ready.

I let the whitefish go before Nolan could gum it to death, then kept fishing until Nolan wore out, sagging in the pack and starting to whimper, naptime chasing hard after him. The slog through the shallows back to the truck kept him occupied, holding the crying at bay until I could get the bottle into him. He slept all the way home.

The next morning we were out even earlier, hoping to beat the heat. Again he slept on the way out, but as soon as I parked beneath the cottonwood he was wriggling wildly, hard to change, hard to get into the pack. He beat his hands against my shoulders when he saw the river again; reached forward to grab handfuls of my hair as I twisted over the barbed wire.

We worked down to the same hole we'd fished the day before, and I picked up where I'd left off, tiny rainbows skittering across the water at the end of my line, Nolan watching silently over my shoulder at the silvery dazzle of water and fish. We worked the hole for an hour, Nolan touching the sides and faces of a dozen little trout, before I moved downstream hoping to find a deeper run, something larger to show him.

He dropped off to sleep on the downstream hike, his head tapping my shoulder with every step. I found the deep run and cast gently, not rocking Nolan, and had a total lack of success. The day was heating up and I turned to give Nolan all the shade I could, but when he woke up he was hot and cramped, and he let me know it. I double-timed upstream, the truck more than a mile away, thinking I'd blown it this time; pushed too far too fast. By the time I reached the original hole, Nolan was having a come-apart. I stopped, swinging the pack into the short, shockingly green, water grass, releasing the straps holding Nolan as quickly as I could. Spreading a blanket, I gave him a bottle, which he worked on feverishly for nearly a minute before he was asleep again, mouth drooped open, milk pooled in the corners.

Providing the only shade for him, I sat anchored. While his breath whistled in and out, I watched him, then the water, then him. The little fish had quit rising, the hatch dead and blown away. I looked at Nolan. Slipping my fly box out of my pocket I tied on a giant grasshopper. They were everywhere. Maybe after a sleep he'd allow me to fish the last stretch back to the truck. We'd been out over two hours now, more even than yesterday. If he didn't let me fish another cast, it was still more than I had ever hoped.

Sitting beside the river, watching Nolan, I couldn't help wondering about all the things my dad had made me worry I might be too old to wonder about. I wondered who Nolan would turn out to be, this tiny kid hidden in the stiff grass, his whole body shaded by just my head. I hoped as he grew that he'd still love water, and fishing, the wind and the hills, all of this. I hoped I'd have the strength to take it if he didn't, the strength not to push, to find what he liked and try it, too—all the stuff I'd wondered about since the first day at the hospital, the sun red behind me on its way down, his mother sleeping in front of me, Nolan's pinched face resting, eyes shut tight, red fingers clamped around my thumb.

When I next glanced at Nolan's face, his eyes were watching me. He took a drink from the bottle I offered, then pulled at the grass, distracted. The smell of mint was thick, and I looked for a leaf to crush for him, but couldn't find any. In the meantime, Nolan found a grasshopper.

Only one hind leg was trapped in Nolan's fist, and when the hopper opened its clattering wings, Nolan let go, pulling his hand toward his mouth, as if the escape itself were something he might be able to taste. He seemed so awake, so himself, I strapped him back in the pack and stepped into the river.

Nolan leaned over the side to watch the water. No kicking anymore, no squirming, just that steady gaze. I stripped out line, the ratcheting making him glance for a moment at the reel before he looked back to the riffle of light. I made one cast across the river to where the little fish had been rising, but the hopper floated by. For no reason, I made my next cast straight upstream. The hopper spun on the edge of the hole, hardly a feeding lane, and I had to strip hard to keep out the slack. After two or three strips the hopper was sucked under by a swirl the tiny rainbows could never have made.

I stripped again and raised the rod tip. The answer through the rod into my hands made me whisper, "Nolan!" Then the fish cut across the stream, giving me a glimpse of its side, and I said, "Nolan, this is a real fish!"

For a few minutes the real fish stayed on the far side of the river, just holding, the rod arced over. Maybe I gave off something Nolan could smell; excitement, fear. Maybe it was only my breathing, so much faster than it'd been a second before, that made Nolan sit straighter. It wasn't until the fish crossed back to our side of the river, dashing upstream and down in short bursts that Nolan began to jump in his pack. The trout was easy to see in the shallow water; a brown, a brown bigger than any I'd ever caught. When the trout was close, leaving a wake, breaking the surface with every shift of direction, Nolan was leaning so far out of the pack I was afraid I'd

ᔑ   *My Heart's First Steps*

forgotten to strap him in. His feet pounded my back—wild kicking his highest expression of joy. When I squatted, trying to keep Nolan upright while I handled the fish, Nolan started to shriek, what Rose calls his raven shouts.

I rolled the brown belly up, working the hopper's hook out of his upper jaw. The trout held still, and though I wanted to let Nolan touch it, its teeth looked too able to shred. Instead I held it up quickly, out of reach, and said, "Nolan, this is the biggest trout I've ever caught in my life," immediately thinking, *So what? They've all been the biggest fish in his life.*

Nolan waved his hands toward the fish, struggling to get closer, to explore this new thing, but I bent down and cradled the fish in the water, stroking its sides until I felt the undeniable surge and the trout shot back into the broken water, disappearing as quickly as it had appeared.

I stood up straight, letting Nolan grab my slimed finger, hoping that would be good enough. I sucked in my breath, my imitation of Nolan's imitation of a raven. Nolan answered, still kicking, and, sticking the hopper's hook into the cork of my rod butt, we splashed through the river on the way home, cawing at each other, Nolan pumping my finger, the river bright in our eyes as I hoped everything for him. 🍂

Sam Listens

Dan Sklar

I want to write about Samuel
and the time he stood
on the front lawn
on a warm April day
and it was six P.M.
and there were birds
and bells and a train
whistle and bees
and a dog and an airplane
and a car and kids playing
and ball bouncing
and wind chimes
and lawn mower and distant
piano and a mother calling
"Ronny!"
A hammering somewhere.

I want to write this poem
to remember the time when
Sam was one year
and three months listening
to these things that
came all at once.
To see Sam in a
white T-shirt,
white diaper, bare feet,
finger pointing to the air,
mouth saying something. 🖤

First Picnic

∽ LIZA HYATT ∽

℗ Seven months old, your first two teeth have come in. Two white sprouts blooming from the ledge of your tender gums, in the same week that the woodland wildflowers with names like toothwort and bloodroot open on the ridge over Tears-of-Joy Creek. I have brought you to see them, brought you out on this bright spring day to show you the world, to show you things you've never dreamed of.

I spread a picnic blanket near the trail, plop you down on it, and you lunge toward the woodland carpet at the blanket's edge. Almost crawling, but not quite, you reach a flower, crunch it in your hand, rip off petals, sit up, and bring them to your mouth. For a long time we play at this. You find flowers, grass, pieces of bark, clumps of dirt, little sticks, an ant, moss. You clutch at the precious riches waiting to be tasted, and I name them for you as I keep you from swallowing them whole. "Oh, you found bark. Yes, that is stone. Yes, that is dirt. All this, and this, you're touching her, our mother Earth."

I open the plastic produce bag full of strawberries. When you see them you say, "Oowuh!" the way you do when you are excited. With both hands wide open you strain toward the berries like someone at a church revival in the midst of an alleluia, like a trapeze acrobat in midair reaching for the next silver swing. I bite the ripe, red tip off the juiciest berry, feed it to you, and lick berry juice and baby spit from my finger. You tongue it for a few seconds, thick red juice oozing out onto your pink lips. Then you swallow, "Oowuh!" and thrust your hands up in another alleluia, another flying-leap request for more. I oblige with a second small bite of berry from my own mouth. It goes down fast, too, and the next and the next.

Finally I give you your own strawberry, a fat one you can easily hold. Like the dirt and the stones and the bark and the flowers, this strawberry is the first. You slobber on it, scrape at it with your new teeth, suck it to a pulp, push it whole into your mouth, spit it back out, cry when I take it away. I mush it up and feed it to you in stringy lumps already partially dissolved by your own saliva. We do this with a second berry and a third. Your hands and face and shirt are covered with red pulp and you look as pleased with your meal as a lion on the Serengeti licking wildebeest blood from her fur. When I look at my watch, an hour has passed just eating strawberries.

When the berries are gone and I've wiped your face, we blow bubbles from a pink plastic wand dipped in soap. They float toward you, spin and eddy in the breeze, reflecting tree branches just coming into leaf, creek, cloud, earth, flower, our own faces, a sun in rainbow paisley skies. Laughing, you touch your first bubble. It pops immediately. Your face changes in the same moment from smiling to serious. You look at me, confused.

Death, I think, appalled at what I've inadvertently shown you.

But you plunge your hands toward the bubble wand, the soap, laughing again, wanting more. I blow another stream toward you. The bubbles waft past. Some burst in midflight. Some are speared by grass, snagged by gentle petals. Some land on your head, brush your cheek, reach your hands. They all pop, they all die. You laugh and cry and laugh as this one pops, then this one, then this. Tears in my eyes, I keep the bubbles coming, watching you learn so quickly, so agreeably, about transience, feeling my heart breaking again and again and again.

"Ephemeral," I whisper to you between blows. "That's what they call these flowers. The ephemerals."

Like you, I used to be in love with everything—with life, with the world and all the little things. But so much that I've loved has been lost. I stopped throwing myself into life like a trapeze artist, stopped falling into love, most of the time trying to find a contented existence in the safety net. As you grow up, you will see my adult stiffness, my fear of things, my hesitancy and rigidity. You will swear that you will never be like me. You will think I am silly, you will be ashamed of me. Someday, when you are much older, we will talk about love, loss, heartache. I hope in this life you will be spared, more than I have been, from losing what doesn't need to be lost. What doesn't need to be lost is the willingness to open to new moments, new loves, even as the past adds up, even as the compost heap outgrows the garden.

Two bluebirds wing by us. One stops on a branch overhanging the creek, then dives away following its mate. I blow you more bubbles, watch them float over the flowers like spherical moths, white butterflies stirred up in a cloud from the ground. I try to see the bubbles from your eyes as well as my own. Like the wildflowers, the soap bubbles are ephemerals. Here one moment, gone the next. Ephemeral flowers. Ephemeral bubbles. Ephemeral leaves.

Ephemeral wind. Ephemeral birds. Ephemeral clouds. Ephemeral trees. Ephemeral me. Ephemeral you.

I've felt an unflagging tug in blood, bone, and nerve from the day you were born. Your father, who is wired differently and will never be awash with mom-hormones, commented casually as we drove home from the hospital, that you might live to vacation on the moon. "Not in our lifetime," he said. "But maybe in yours." I was in the backseat guarding over you, as you sat curled up in the huge carseat looking as small as a thimble in a soup tureen. Tears filled my eyes and my throat knotted up. At that moment, it was a total surprise and shock to be told that we wouldn't spend every moment of forever together.

That is what I see watching the bubbles float over the forest floor's flowers. The whole ephemeral universe going up in smoke with you and I in it, bubbles inside of bubbles, expanding, living, stretching, until poof! it's all over except for a brief rain of soap spray, as the shape of life as we know it breaks apart, scatters, evaporates.

From your perspective, the bubbles come and go, come and go, magically. You aren't thinking about past, future, compost, garden, life, death. You aren't thinking about the soap bubble universe's expansion and dissolution. You are in the universe and of the universe and that is all.

Amidst a stream of bubble galaxies, a double bubble—two partial spheres, large and small, attached as one—emerges from the bubble wand. It floats between us, drifts toward the picnic blanket. "There *we* are," I say. The double bubble lands on the blanket, lingers awhile, then silently quivers, folds, and disappears. You see this and forget it as a new bubble floats up to kiss your cheek. You reach for it, wobble, and regain balance.

Watching you, I suddenly feel freed, able to see this very moment as it is, a bubble saying, "This is life. Hello, good-bye! Pop!" and the next moment is already here with its own kiss of hello, good-bye. And pop, pop, pop, pop, the moments keep coming and going and so you and I are here, laughing at how it is all so beautiful and so short, and I want to say to you, "So this is how it's done! Alleluia!" as the next silver moment swings toward us and we catch hold and let go and fall, flying into the next. "This is how to love. Fall into life and out. In and out of love and in and out with each passing second." But I can see from the bright gleam in your eyes that your body, your whole being is on fire with such loving. All along it has been you who are showing me the world, showing me things I've never dreamed of. You are overflowing with holy spirit and I kneel before you, dragging crutches, safety net behind, having come to this revival to be healed. 🦋

Jacob's Ladder

CLARK KAROSES

Warm bathwater twists from the tap. You sit
up to your shoulders as steam peels from our heads
and examine the cliché, but blue, rubber duck—
turning it around and upside-down, meticulous
with those tiny, heat-ruddy hands, rubbing it
along your gums to feel it squeak
across budding teeth, trying to grasp the whole of it.
Your pudgy cheeks are dumbstruck by the simple
thingness of things. As though pained
with a sudden need, a fresh intent, you let the duck drop
into bubbles, reach for the warm stream falling in
and try to draw it toward you—like some
clear baton you might wield and handle.

But your wide eyes find that it eludes the grip
you'd learned to trust and slips through the fingers.
You look to me, half-smiling with befuddlement, wonder,
fright—grab again, look again, and in my face see
that it is as it's supposed to be,
and go on trying to grab and grab and grab.

And this is just one of the realizations
I hope are many and early in your climb
out of the angelic confusion of youth.
Just one of the *Eureka!*s on your way
to greatness, or happiness, or something else.
I pray you find the ladder not so difficult
and shifty as I've found it or made it,
hammering my bias, crooked sticks
to the main. I pray your ladder reaches
the clearest, widest vistas—not this
soggy interior of cloud. And I pray, finally,
that you take it slow, find good footing,
and don't climb too high only to find yourself
on insubstantial rungs that slither from your step
or squeeze between your fingers. ♥

Step

∞ JOYCE M. FISCHER ∞

☯ How else could it have been?

You wobbled all summer at the farmhouse in Umbria, sat like a Buddha before della Francescas and Giottos, crawled through fields of lavender and rosemary, picking up fresh figs every morning for your breakfast. You held the waiter's pant leg and wouldn't take a step for the blood-orange gelato he offered with his long, slender hands. You sat and smiled and let the shop ladies bring you the princess puppet, the stuffed giraffe, the chocolate flower, never deigning to stand. You held out your small hands and Italy came to you.

When we packed in September, you made your decision. You stood and rushed into Roberto's arms, not one first step but eight of them, straight to the most beautiful man in Italy. From then on he was yours, and so was the world.

That night, I stood on the Roman stone bridge and watched the moonrise over the hills. I couldn't close my eyes without seeing your face. I wept the oldest tears in creation, the tears of a mother who has taught her child to be strong and full of grace, and most important of all, to walk away from her. ⚘

Savanna Stalling

TODD W. PALMER

We say *Look*
And her eager eyes follow our fingers
She listens hard to what is pointed out
But ignores our silly labels—
Tree Bird Cloud
As if she doesn't want any words
To get in her way

And somewhere in the miles
Of videotape we've shot
I captured proof she said *Da-da* first—
Of course *Ma-ma* soon followed
But three months have passed
And she's no longer
Calling us by name
Maybe she's onto something—

Since names force separation
Mother from Father
Ocean from Sky
Why not leave it all connected untitled

I sit at my desk
Mulling over metaphor
Trying to piece it all back together
But Savanna has no use
For simile or symbol
Because everything together as one
Just *is*

Perhaps she's stalling
And I don't blame her
Language can wait

Words tend to get uglier with age—
Responsibility Decision Hysterectomy

Each first for our last child
Is a final first for us
So we want to play
This waiting game as well
No reason to rush her
To walk talk and run
No need to label
This stalling as Love. 🐛

My Heart's First Steps

When You Are Ready, Climb

James P. Lenfestey

You hug your mother like a life vest
and shun me like deep water.

She saved your life.
At the first instance of your birth,
she knew you were too blue.
She woke you up, the doctor, me.
You were both so frightened then,
you cling to each other now
as if there were no gravity.

I wait, rooted,
casting the sun in winter,
shade in summer.
When you are ready,
climb.

Pull my branches.
Crack my limbs.
Strip my leaves.
My roots are deep.
As I am tall.
As wide as I am big.

When you are ready,
climb. 🌱

Father's Day

∾ GUY REED ∾

I opened my eyes. I had been somewhere in my sleep, a distant land, perhaps with a king, riding with privilege in an automobile, but that was gone. What remained was the language of this Sunday morning's awakening: the birds already singing for half an hour, the young cat meowing at the windowsill, and the rain. The same rainfall I first heard gush from the sky with a thunder clap, waking me just after midnight with the panicked thought, "The car windows are down." Most things I'd let go, roll over, return to sleep, even laundry on the line sometimes, but open windows in a downpour was not one of them. So I hopped out of bed, flipped the switch of the outdoor floodlight, slipped my flip-flops on, and went outside in my striped underwear.

The first couple of rain pelts felt surprising on my back, but after rolling up the windows I just stood there, splatters of mud collecting on my heels. It had been very hot for three days straight and the warm rain felt good. While standing in the driveway watching the silhouettes of rain streaking through the light, I began to think about my father. I thought about some of the things my father had told me about myself, including that I didn't possess enough sense to come in from the rain.

I've always loved taking walks in the rain. Long ago I abandoned the impulse to run from it. "No sense panicking," I reasoned, "after all, it's simple rain, not burning lava, why scurry? I'll dry." I've never owned an umbrella. It always seemed like one thing too many, especially when I already had a coat and a hat.

When my daughter came along and then learned to walk, I was happy she loved to be outdoors. She rarely got cold. And even though she played with lots of dolls and would wear only dresses, I was glad that she liked to overturn rocks and wasn't afraid to pick up worms, slugs, or salamanders. She was always so kind in moving the little orange newts to the safety of the roadside. She loved being out in the rain. Most rainy days my wife or I would hear the screen door close and go look after her from the window. Our little girl would be outside with her shiny face raised to the sky, arms, palms, and fingers stretched wide, her long blond curls straightening with the weight of the water gathering there.

Down at the end of the driveway, near the yellow mailbox and the blue stone fence, off to the side where I let the weeds, wildflowers, and grass grow tall, there was a four-foot-wide depression between the irises and the gravel road. The low spot there could be dry for weeks or even months, but with a good rainfall the water collected, creating a little pond for a few days, maybe a week or so, and as if by magic, a frog would be in the pond. My daughter and I would see it there when going out to play. We'd crouch to watch it swim and then, taking turns it seemed, the frog would sit off to the edge of the iris stalks while the naked three-year-old girl jumped and splashed in the puddle with her red rubber boots. I loved that frog. Sometimes, when getting the mail or taking a walk during a dry spell, I'd check the little depression and grass, but I never did see the frog. "How?!" I wondered. The nearest water was 170 feet underground.

I stood in the rain the first few minutes of Father's Day, wondering if there were magic seedling tadpoles in some of the falling raindrops. I then wondered whether or not my father had received the greeting card I mailed to him. I had spent much of my boyhood fishing with my father. The card, a photo of a trout cut to the shape of the fish, wished him a *Happy Father's Day!* Inside the card, I thanked him for his honest effort. I wasn't sure my father would understand what I meant. I wasn't sure I knew either, but I knew he'd ask. Anyway, I'd give him a call later. I was tired, it was the middle of the night, and I was out in the rain.

I went back inside the house. I wanted to spend the day with my family, looked forward to it, but I still felt the need to be alone for a time. My daughter had recently begun to ask questions I couldn't answer, couldn't answer for the world, couldn't answer for her or even for myself. I didn't know what to do about that quite yet. I turned off the outdoor light, put on a T-shirt, and returned to bed, the sheets already damp from the humidity. Maybe I didn't have sense enough to come in from the rain, and maybe now my daughter didn't either, but I would never tell her that. Some folks just love rain. Besides, I was beginning to believe that magic frogs grow in puddles. Drifting back to sleep, I heard it begin to rain hard and I knew I'd find another frog, or the same one again, later in the day with my daughter, near the end of our yard, the edge of the known world. 🍂

Ah . . .

JOHN HOLBROOK

there she is
my sweet
one
butter plum
of a
daughter
pumpkin
plump
bright
in her
yellow
cotton pumps
sipping
with a straw
a rainbow
if you please
in spray
where our sprinkler
falls

her nice
white socks
soaked
in fresh
clipped grass
her grin
twinkles in
her eyes . . .

Ah, I see
now
what she
intends to hold
me hostage to
in this life.

Christmas Shopping with Preschoolers

HELENE BARKER KISER

At the bookstore I promise we'll go to the
    children's section
as soon as I'm finished looking, not browsing
    like I want to,

just scanning the shelves for the precise
    books I came for, nothing
else; the kids take coats off, drop them in the
    aisle, tug my arm, tug

shelved books, punctuate the clock's tick of
    each five seconds gone by
without my finishing as promised with *You
    ready now, Mom?*

until I give up, head for the children's
    section, kids shrieking
ahead at full speed, struggle to be patient and
    in control—

My Heart's First Steps

they grab books off the shelves
	indiscriminately, make a pile
on the floor which becomes many piles and
	I pray no pages

rip, cursing myself for having brought them
	in the first place, choke
down screams, urge the kids off the shelves
	they're climbing *Not a jungle*

gym urge them to the checkout *Not a*
	playground where they circle
angel ornament and calendar displays *you*
	can't get me

I win I win and I try to catch them without
	losing my
place in line, try to jam coat sleeves on arms
	suddenly both limp

and rigid, wrestle against the flurry of limbs,
	triumphant blue eyes,
until it's my turn, bodies jerking and jiggling
	right next to

me without moving and I'm a penny short,
	ignore my son's
tug, his words I don't hear, accept a penny
	from the woman

My Heart's First Steps

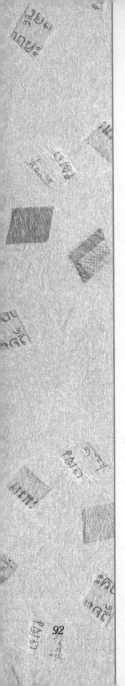

next to me gratefully, hand it to the cashier
    gratefully,
who smiles at me I think gratefully, so I can
    turn to see

my son, whose voice is now a wail, whose
    pants, underwear, puddle
around his ankles *because my bottom's hurting*
    tears spilling

like milk, blue eyes bright as a new penny,
    pale bottom and white
legs lit under fluorescents because he
    doesn't yet know shame,

pure in his need, my arms, before knowledge
    finds him ripped loose, eyes
steeled, not really blue but hazel green, the
    color of my own.

Husbandry

DANE CERVINE

When a man lays down his life
for his family
when he says
> *you have all that I am*

When a man eviscerates his soul
peeled open like a deer
for the eager mouths of his children
when he says
> *eat my bone marrow*
> *sip from my heart*
> *sate your hunger deep in my body*

When a man labors
far into the evening with his wife
bringing order to the house
fallen prey to storms and monsoons
blowing wildly through the limited hours
when he stays still in the quiet of the last hour
> *fold your longing deep in my arms*

You know he is in love   with his living
you know his spirit   lurking like a monk
cloistered in the monastic   cell
is descending from the tower   to the town
is finding his beloved deity   incarnate
in the terrestrial life that   swallows him   whole

as though   the gnostic breach

in the cosmic fabric
between matter and light
were sewn together with   carnal thread
                                transfigured

as though God   peeking
through the man's eyes
into his inconsequential days
were saying
　　I have found my life in yours. 🌑

Brushing Teeth

∾ PAUL VOS BENKOWSKI ∾

⊚ There was a time when I dreamt of becoming a college professor, a dream my parents shared with me, and I encouraged them in it. I don't know where this ambition disappeared to, but I remember it this morning. I close my eyes and I am standing in front of a small, alert audience of students with their notebooks open and pens at the ready, waiting for my eloquent delivery of penetrating insights into the works of Dostoyevsky and Saramago and the like. You know, going on and on about why *Something Happened* by Joseph Heller is the greatest American novel ever written, and I would be more than willing to patiently argue down anyone who thought otherwise.

Then I open my eyes, still this morning, and I stare into the mirror as I brush my teeth standing over our second son, Soren, who is eighteen months old and trying valiantly to brush his teeth as well. He only chews on his older brother's toothbrush. I have not showered in days, I am wearing the same clothes that I slept in, I have not shaved in more than a week, I have deep, dark bags under my eyes, and yet I think of that dream I once had. Why now? Maybe it is the Gogol book by Nabakov that sits on top of the toilet tank, or maybe it's a rare moment of clarity, but as I guide Soren through the oh-so-important rinsing and spitting cycle of tooth brushing, I cannot help but begin the morning's discussion, while he looks up at me and wonders if what I'm suddenly saying has anything to do with dental care. It does not, I assure him. Then I start the day's lesson, in which we will discuss the epilepsy of Prince Myshkin, and how one should not concern oneself with Dostoyevsky's own battles with epilepsy because, as we all well know from previous lessons, the *life* of the artist is accidental, the *work* of the artist is not.

The life of a parent is not accidental. There are no accidental births. Semen properly placed inside a woman's vagina can cause pregnancy! Fortunately we understood this, my wife and I, and we both wanted to be parents, though I never gave it much thought. When I did consider it, I was thinking of far-off days playing catch with a five-year-old. Or I was teaching a teenager how to drive a car. Or I was playing guitar with a young adult, discussing sevenths and augmented sixths. Never did I imagine scrubbing a cloth diaper, or watching with worry and horror my fifteen-month-old being anes-thetized for minor surgery. So quickly did those previous daydreams vanish, and so clear are the realities.

I do play catch with our sons, and I watch them drive around on tricycles, waving bye-bye as they pretend to drive off to work, or to the store, or to the museum. And they both have stopped me while playing guitar so that they can tune, strum, and warble a song them-selves. These events please me more than any fantasy could.

I never completed college. I dropped out. I still remember three professors from my short stay and I have frank and open discussions with each of them, wherever they may be, which is wherever I may be. Like at the park, alternating between two swinging swings, giving an under-duck or two, then asking one of my professors, the great Davy Carozza, to stop going on about Italo Calvino and tell me more about his days in Italy during WW II when he carried a rifle for the resistance. The boys might turn to me and wonder who I am speaking to, but they are busy with their own minds, gathering in all that can be gathered from the sound of the wind rushing by their ears to the whys of why do we have eyebrows, to concern themselves with my quiet ramblings. I have learned freedom from them. Freedom of the imagination, openness to the world. There is no inside or outside to their minds. There is nothing private or sacred. I have learned by watching them sing songs out loud while walking down the street; from listening to our oldest carry on at great length with one of his imaginary friends. So what if their papa spends his days mumbling to himself about bread recipes or songs or what to write down on thesis pages? It means to them what it means to me: nothing!

Maybe someday they will ask me what I am saying and I will have to tell them the truth, which is that I think that I am a college professor, and for your next assignment, you have to read Part One of *The Idiot* and be ready to discuss why this is the finest opening of any book you will ever have the chance to read. Then we will dance to a do-you-remember album until it is time for naps.

Perhaps it is childlike of me to go on pretending that I am a college professor. But my parents are proud of me in my alternate reality, one of thesis and composition and talk of tenure. Of course in this reality, they will never know that I am a professor, not unless they eavesdrop during some visit and hear me carrying on while brushing Soren's teeth, showing him, so young, just how rich we all can be. ❦

Fatherhood

Dan Sklar

Sometimes, on a Saturday afternoon,
you feel *adult,* especially after
managing to get the crib upstairs.
Your five-year-old is in the bath,
your wife is holding the baby, and
later you are all going (including
your mother-in-law) to an art
opening in Boston. You have to
go, because the artist is your wife's
friend who is getting divorced,
and it's her birthday. She wants
you all to be there so you have
to go. Chopin's on the radio, and
you like it. You like movies from
the sixties, like *Mr. Hobbs Takes
a Vacation.* You take pleasure in
vacuuming and mopping and raking
leaves and mowing the lawn and
smoking cigars (outside). Still,

your mother sends you an ad for a
nationally advertised poetry contest and
writes, "What have you got
to lose?" You have an office with
memories of people that have been in your office.
They sat right in that chair, and
told you things, and you thought
things you would not tell anyone.
You listen to Jackie Gleason's
greatest hits and it relaxes you. You
love how your son sings "Summer
Wind" and listens to Frank Sinatra
and remembers the words. You
join the Massachusetts Audubon
Society and actually go bird
watching. You and your sons see
four deer at the bird sanctuary.
This is the life you wanted. 🐦

Walking with Your Son

PETER KROK

Now walking these pavements with your son
in his Big Wheel clattering on the cement,
you stop to browse outside the windows
of his morning kindergarten classroom.
Then he finds a ledge and jumps onto your back
piggybacking on the ladder of your shoulders.
He picks up chestnuts and left over maple wings
and stores them in your swelling pockets,
his curios of nature, like the fireflies
of a month ago he put inside his mayonnaise jar.

Now, by the lamp in the evening,
as he lies under his covers,
you want to hold the hour in your hands
but instead you have a chestnut
and upstairs the breath of your boy. ❦

Enlightenment Begins at Home

DANE CERVINE

Riding along in the car
on a family outing Norman Rockwell
would have been proud of

there are moments like this

Gabriel my three-year-old
surveys the scene

breaks out in a big smile
and sings

family family family

laughter all around—
time standing still.

If Buddha had known
such enlightenment

would he have stayed
homc

could there be anything
out there

worth more? ❦

Break

∾ JENNIFER GRAF GRONEBERG ∾

⊙ It is the late spring morning of an ordinary day and I am putting the laundry away, clean clothes still warm from the dryer folded in a tower in my arms. I have just kissed my husband, Tom, good-bye, on his way out the door to town, twelve miles away. Our black-and-white border collie, Truman, dashes past me, trying to escape the small, half-dressed boy running around the house with no pants on. Carter, our son. The woodstove glows against the spitting snow outside. The forecast is for a blizzard. I am wondering if winter will never end, thinking of that T. S. Eliot line about April being the cruelest month, when I hear a snap like the crack of dry wood, only there is no wood that could snap like that, then I hear crying coming from our bedroom, cries like none I'd ever heard before.

I drop the clothes, everything coming undone. I rush to our bedroom, to Carter, who is rolling slowly on the floor, mewling, whimpering. I race to the window and pound on it, trying to get Tom's attention before he drives away with our car. He sees me. I race back to Carter, try to hold him, ask him what's wrong, *what's wrong, baby, what's wrong*. He can't speak from the pain.

Clothes, it's impossible to find clothes. I grab pants for Carter from the laundry on the floor, but can't find socks. I give him mine, *owie, owie, rockie rockie Mommy*, then Carter crawls into our big bed, asking *hold me*.

Owie owie Mommy, Carter points to his right shin. I grab a package of frozen peas to use as an ice pack and Tom drives us all to the hospital. Carter is looking out the window and he is not crying, he is turning in to himself, maybe going into shock. Tom drives faster. We make it to the ER where the receptionist is talking on the phone, seemingly unconcerned about the toddler I carry in my arms, our ice pack of frozen peas. I try to get her attention, cough, stomp my feet, but there is no blood, nothing obvious for her to see. "Excuse me," Tom says to her, and she notices us finally. We are shown to a room and a man in blue-green scrubs asks us what happened, asks how. I don't know any of the answers.

We need X-rays. We leave our things piled neatly, my socks taken from Carter's feet, Tom's baseball cap, the frozen peas. I hold Carter, because it is the only way he can do this, he is scared and the machine is big and the technician keeps telling us he will shoot us quickly. "Tell me a story," Carter manages, and I do, I tell him the never-ending bedtime story about the boy with a mommy and a daddy and a black-and-white dog who live in a magical forest, only I don't know how this story will go.

We return to the exam room, back to our small pile of belongings, and wait. I continue the story, telling of the brave boy who lived in the magical forest, of the time the boy went to the hospital to have a picture of his leg taken by a magic machine that could show us our bones inside, big and strong, the bones of a boy. The doctor shows us the X-rays and I think that the last time I'd seen these grainy, gray-and-black images was Carter's ultrasound. His tiny fingers were curled in a fist and the dots of the bones in his spine looked like a string of pearls. Now we see another image. Here are the bones of the lower leg; here is where the tibia snapped.

Dave sets the cast. He is a slim, middle-aged Asian man with a silver hoop in his left ear and a long, salt-and-pepper ponytail. He has kind eyes and chapped hands. He pulls out a tray, rolls of gauze in foil, packages of fiberglass for casts, and I think, *so many owies.* Hands, Carter's in mine, so small. Three years, no big hurts. My whole existence had been about avoiding this moment, about protecting him. The plastic plugs in the sockets, our coffee table gone because the corners were too sharp, the bed gone because the slats were dangerous, gates at the stairs, a fence around the woodstove. We'd built a world of soft edges and rounded corners all to protect him, and yet, here we are.

Carter's cast is purple, the color of a grape gumball. On the way home we stop at the hamburger place, *cheeseburger, fries, Daddy soda,* all yeses, anything he wants. At home, I carry him to the house and think how delicate he is, how small and light as a breeze. I need courage, need to be strong, but I feel shaky and scared, off-balance. Everything is suspect. I put Carter on the couch and put in a video about garbage trucks and go to get him a *chocolate milky.* The light is out in the fridge and this frightens me, as if the burned-out bulb is a sign, some portent of more bad things to come. The weather has worsened. The gray, slanting afternoon sunlight hurts Carter's eyes and I pull the shades down. Pain medicine every two hours. Carter sleeps on the couch, me in the big chair next to him. We hold hands.

There are bottles in a line along the kitchen windowsill—

prescription Tylenol with codeine, children's Tylenol, children's ibuprofen. Tylenol for me. An African violet in a yellow pot next to all the medicines. A glass dish containing Carter's frog soap and a bar of sage soap from my mother-in-law, Joyce. A trial-sized lotion for extra-dry hands. My dear, sweet boy.

"I got tangled in the rocking chair, Mommy," I find out later, when the pain is under control and when Carter can speak about it. The chair is the one I picked out with my dad before we even knew the baby I was carrying would be a boy, would be Carter. "You'll be spending a lot of time in this chair," my dad had said, "so it better be comfortable." We tried out all the chairs in the furniture store and picked the best one, the plushest and the most expensive. I ask Tom to move it into the garage. I can't bear to look at it.

The next day phone calls come, people hearing of our trouble and wanting to help. Wendy sends Craig over to plow out our driveway in case we need to get back to town. I make gypsy soup and try to pick up the house, finding solace in the ordinariness of housework. I put more laundry in the dryer to tumble. I bake a chicken, my friend's recipe that she calls whole-house chicken, because your whole house smells like supper. These are the small things I can do.

When the weather finally breaks, gifts arrive from friends, Grandma and Grandpa. A new Lite-Brite, fresh Play-Doh, a lap-sized easel. Videos, a pinwheel, bubbles. E-mails with suggestions to get a beanbag chair so Carter can sit up, use a Radio Flyer wagon to pull him around. I wrap the cast in an Ace bandage, so the skin on his other leg doesn't get scratched by the purple fiberglass. All the stuffed animals break their legs, and Carter wraps them up in Ace bandages. Mommy wears one, too, Daddy also. We are a broken-legged bunch, a family of walking wounded.

Tom and I count days again like we did during pregnancy, only this time it's the number of weeks until the cast comes off. And then one day it is all over, done, the cast no longer needed, and we sit in the exam room again. The break is not completely healed, the doctor explains; the last step in making it stronger is to take the cast off and start walking. It is time for trust now, time for faith in the simple fact of bone knitting to bone, time to believe in the healing power of broken things made right. "No," Carter says. He doesn't want to give it up. The broken leg has become part of him, accepted into his life like so many things he quietly accepts, like when we say, "No more bottles," or, "No more diapers," or, "This is your new baby-sitter." And now he's afraid. Getting the cast off means everything will change again.

"We'll come back when you're ready," I say, though this means more waiting, another appointment in this very busy office, but it is fine. "Fine," I say.

Carter looks at me, then at Dave the cast man, then says, "No, Mommy. It's okay. We can do it today. It's okay." I look at him and again think how small he is, how light. I am so proud of him, my brave boy. All he needed was the chance to decide what would happen to him; all he wanted was to have some say in what came next. ❧

Ode to Lammy Chop

TODD W. PALMER

After she fought like a bear
To be born first   tight-fisted
thirty-six seconds before her sister's first breath,
Bailey had a choice to make.
From the steady sunshower of birth gifts
Gold spoons   silver chalices
Numbered statuary   satin linens
A kingdom of stuffed animals
Parading in two-by-two,

She chose you
A second-hand lamb
Offered by a needful child
Who had nothing more to give
Than what matters most—
Bailey Bear's first round pick
For security purposes.

You've proven your worth,
Suffering strangulation
When she can't conjure words to capture thoughts
Too profound for words.

You've taken the carsick bullet   deflected projectile vomit
With fleece once white as snow—
Honorable sponge soaking it up.
For thanks you were dumped in the dark load
But you held on as she did
Blue-hued and bearhug tight
Through hospital dramas—
Tucked in unable to duck the needles.

Your tail's long gone   bit off
In a one-sided dogfight
Your nap's grown nappy
Spin-cycled by wet beds   kindergarten lice.
Five years have passed
Since the night we performed for Bearsy.

My Heart's First Steps

I made you move above her crib
Played Gepetto too well.
Her giggles bubbled the air until
You seemed too real.
A bolt of fear hurled
By those she trusted most
Jolted her smile taut like the line
She'd drawn between those with and without breath.

On this Thanksgiving's day
Please know, battle-scarred bearer
Of Bailey burdens,
I forgive you for that
And wish on the bone to grant you life again
Pinocchio rights   to play my part
Safeguard the sacred path to her heart
When I can't get there first. 🖤

Grand

T. W. BERRY

Little gypsy woman
at the piano.

Her hair curls softly
pianissimo

round her preschooler
plump perfect face.

Esmeralda earrings
dangling, clashing

beautifully with 101
Dalmatians soiled shirt.

Baby Mine I play
singing those sweet

mother words; she
reaches her tiny bow

mouth for me to kiss,
to remember, to reprise.

Bath Time

∾ ROGER CODY ∾

Most evenings the boys get a bath. Being healthy boys of two and four, they naturally need a bath; but if they didn't, we might well give them one anyway. It's a time for them to have fun, and hopefully, exhaust themselves. The concept of winding down is alien to them—the day's not over until it's over—and by instinct, they race along in top gear until they crash. The bath is therefore a buffer between the day and night, a kind of cleaning-up-and-down-shifting-nightcap.

The bathroom is well equipped. Around the tub are enough animals to stock an ark, although the number of frogs and yellow rubber ducks are in a proportion that Noah would never have permitted. Sharks, squids, and whales are also aboard; to say nothing of soaps, sponges, brushes, cups, bottles, shampoos, lotions, and a library of soft-covered plastic books. High on the walls at opposite ends of the tub are infrared lamps—necessary in the winter, but used the entire year for their cozy ruby-red ambience.

The boys play here differently than they do elsewhere. Perhaps the water excites something in their blood, evoking old memories of Japan or Rome; or perhaps it is merely that they are naked and in water, a combination that excites an ancient and primitive sense of rapture. Whatever it is, they frolic more freely in water. They're more likely to sing and shout in the tub, managing with just two voices to create a hubbub reminiscent of a crowded beach.

They didn't always enjoy bath time: it once held a terror for both of them. To shampoo Philip's hair we'd resort to holding his head over the sink. Clifton sometimes became so hysterical we'd wash him with a sponge. But how they've evolved! Philip now blows bubbles in the water, proving he's long passed the stage where he'd refuse to get his face wet. Clifton tries to copy him, unfortunately, since he's not yet gotten the hang of exactly when to inhale. But when his earnest efforts leave him choking, he's only momentarily deterred. With a look that mixes outrage, chagrin, and consternation, he gets his breath and tries again.

When the bath is over, they typically plead to stay longer, sometimes preventing access to the drain plug with desperate body blocks, and in extreme instances, remain lying on the dry tub bottom after the water has been removed. In the more egregious cases, I use brute force, lifting them up and out of the tub as they flail their arms and legs defiantly. (Just before applying brute force, I usually give them a choice, like, "Which one is coming out first?" Then they can save face by scrambling to be the first for what a moment earlier neither wanted.)

Sometimes I take a bath with them. This changes things for all of us. I get to play with my children in an unusual setting. Invariably they react with enthusiasm when Mom tells them Dad's about to join in. But curiously, they also show a marked sense of solemnity, as if my participation were not only rare, but a privilege. This surprises me, because I'm not usually accorded this much overt respect.

According to what's become ritual, I enter the tub by screaming with pain, not entirely feigned, at how hot the water is. Philip gets to say that it's not hot for him. "I'm used to it!" he says in a singsong way that shows he not only knows his part, but is pleased to play it. "Used to it!" echoes Clifton, with typical eager agreement. As for me, I continue to make exaggerated complaints, making the appropriate shrieks of discomfort while they laugh gleefully at their father's inferiority. The tub has equalized us, and we can now proceed as peers.

But being the peer of two small boys is incompatible with bathing. As I protest that I want to soap myself, the two of them, who only after considerable negotiation have agreed to move to the other end of the tub, take turns jumping on me and solicitously pouring water over me, in what they perceive as a beneficial service. "Do you like that, Daddy?" Philip asks, his voice full of concern for this personal service. "Like it?" asks Clifton, pouring water into my nose. Their mother comes over to watch and expresses a similar thought. "They're yours!" she says, meaning it.

The exit ritual is simpler. We've all been in the bath together; now we'll all leave it together. And the togetherness continues. "Dress me!" says Philip, insisting that I not leave him. "Me, too," shouts Clifton, also wishing to maintain our closeness. And so after dressing myself, I towel them off and put them in their nightclothes. Not infrequently, as I hold Philip so that I can put on his pajamas, his body still warm from the bath, he'll say with quiet sincerity, "I love you, Daddy!"

"I love you, too," I tell him.

The sincerity lingers, and Philip expands on his sentiment.

"I love you more than you love me!" he asserts.

"Impossible!" I say.

"I love you five hundred dollars!" he responds, quantifying the matchless capacity of his affection.

"Five dollars!" says Clifton, still with us and trying to wriggle out of his towel.

"I love you more than there are dollars in the world!" I say, escalating my bid.

At this point Philip may invent something entirely original, and utterly touching. "I love you more than everything!" he's said, or, stretching up both hands, "I love you more than the whole sky!" Whatever the expression, the sentiment is his own. He doesn't overdo it—soon he'll be disobeying me as is his wont—but for the moment, he seems to be responding to the bath and the experience of sharing it with me.

But Philip is growing up. After he swims at the Y these days, he takes a shower in the locker room. And although he seems to enjoy the sensuous thrill of a hot shower as much as the sybaritic bliss of a hot bath, I can see that the days of the bath are numbered. At least until he's a father, and he, too, can bathe with his offspring. If he's fortunate, perhaps they'll let him dry and dress them, and in the warm afterglow of a good soak, tell him they love him more than the whole sky. ♥

Still Life with Children

TARA MOGHADAM

I keep children near at hand to hear things,
the way trees nail the mountain,
the lament of a cloud,
the interpretation of the dog's dream.

Who else would ever ask me—
Why do we live in houses?
Why doesn't snow melt into milk?
Where does God go when he just wants to sing?

We come to picnic. Nearby a young river gurgles
like a baby with incessant wet gibberish.

I motion for the children to rest their heads
against their hands, to close their eyes.
We take a moment to shed skins to another world.

After the quiet, we open our eyes to a miracle
of color, every shade of red alive in the bounding sway
of anemones holding tight to the long end of stem.

My Heart's First Steps

The children giggle. They want to eat them.
Soon they have gathered seeds, broken stems,
    pulled petals.
They want to pick flowers and give them to
    everyone they meet.
To cover the whole world with crimson delight.

I watch their heads bob and sway as they paint
pollen onto each other's cheeks and chatter.
I know they can do this all well before dinner. 🌿

My Heart's First Steps

The Playground

∽ Rebecca Balcarcel ∽

The floor is a layer of shredded wood chips four inches deep. Our footfalls make a sound I remember from hiking under evergreens, the *crick-crack* of thick mats of pine needles. The boys march and stomp, trying out the ground's give. They shout and call to one another, then scamper off to explore. Later, when my oakshade has passed over the bench, they reach the late stage, the no-hands-off-the-roof-of-the-playhouse, the down-the-slide-on-your-back-headfirst stage. I think of all the toys I have tired of: sex, would you believe it? TV, movies. I can see they have tried every permutation of slide and every combination of boys-chase-girls-chase-boys. Matthew has played "Matthew climbing the tower," "Matthew spinning," and "Matthew upside down." Now he is ready to be just Matthew again, and with him the twins come running to me, looking for a place to rest. One has scraped his heel, another his shin, nothing that won't heal. I look down to see the three of them (my God!) happy, satisfied, and content. They shine, beaming, "I have felt the ladder rung in the arch of my foot. I have heard the sound of sticks clattering down the slide. I have seen tree bark an eyelash-length away. I have done it. I am it." With their hearts still glowing, I am seeing them. I walk with them in their light all the way home. 🌿

My Days Are Made of You and Me

KAREN HOWLAND

You dance tangerine slices across my skin, singing I
    love Mama.
Your cheeks burst with citrus juice, the sun runs down
    your chin.

Anticipation is too much, you eat cheese right through the
    wrap.
Your first embrace of everything captivates me completely.

Your feet leave the certainty of gravity, jubilant, jump, leap,
spilling into my lap, I quiet you with a kiss, and you're off

flying, feeling, falling the fruit of you, the tree of me,
    we spin
spring, rise, unravel, lose track of what never mattered

telling time by milk rather than clocks. We smell heaven
in cinnamon and pillows and small corners the world
    forgets.

There is a melon slice in your open palm, an orange smile
That travels from your hand, to open lips, to my soul. ❧

This Is the Life

Dan Sklar

This is the life
Sammy says. We're
in the hammock

nothing like it
this spring
Saturday the

trees are treeing
kids are kidding
leaves are leafing

breeze, breezing
fence, fencing
sky, skying

the cool, cooling
the blue, bluing
flowers are flowery.

An aroma in the air
reminds me of spring
when I was a kid and

will remind Sam of
when he was a kid
when he grows up.

I close my eyes
on this hammock
on this happiness

open them, see Sam
and leaves and sky
dream of words
and jazz, someone

speaking Spanish
in the distance.

We float and drift
and dream in this
hammock, this
happiness. I love
how Sammy says *Dad*.

He will have his
dad on this spring
hammock, this
spring happiness. ❦

My Heart's First Steps

The Digging Hole

∞ Anna Viadero ∞

At the edge of our yard, where the mossy lawn is swallowed by forest, my boys have a digging hole. The ground gives easily to their efforts with tablespoons, plastic shovels, or long-handled hoes. The soil is Connecticut river-bottom sand, and when they shiver it with broad spades or bare hands, they are prospecting through layers of time. I can almost hear them loose the thunder of long-gone dinosaurs, or see their heads cock to the sound of the leather-bound steps of Pocumtuck warriors.

This hole is laced with tangible treasures, too. Animal bones, chips of Blue Willow china, a skein of rusted wire. Chunks and shards of deep red brick, manufactured on our land when a masonry stood where our home is. They find railroad spikes, or large squares of aged, opaque glass, whose once-sharp edges are now just smooth memory. From the kitchen window over the sink, I hear them put into that hole as much as they take out.

When Dominic, my anxious, younger son was about to start preschool, he and his older brother Jason, who'd already been through it, dug the hole big. After it was big enough for two to sit inside, Jason took a crooked twig and drew the preschool. He drew its horseshoe driveway, its sticky screen door, and the entrance wall of cubbies. He drew the snack area, the listening space, and the sinks. On Dom's first day of school, he calmly claimed the space his brother had shown him.

When Jason came home with bruised shins in the third grade, Dom offered him a dose of raw power. He filled the hole with leaves and they swung high on a nearby rope, flying off at peak-swing and jumping cleanly into the leaf-softened pit.

At eight and ten now, they dig in more complex ways. At the start of Jason's sex education curriculum, I heard them howl and fall and roll beside the hole, as they threw all the wild names they could think of for men's private parts deep into it. They laughed till they couldn't breathe.

Our friends swear the hole is a liability. My husband or I will break our neck in it, they say, walking our dog at dark. I smile. I know that in a very short while, when my kids are grown and gone, I will go to that hole and lean in toward its center, where the memory of my boys' growing is stored. 🌿

My Heart's First Steps

Next Steps

A Boy on a Beach

∽ TERRENCE DUNN ∽

You walk ahead of me, head down and arms held tightly across your chest. We have just gotten done screaming at each other, our faces inches apart. Now you turn and walk off, leaving me alone on my knees with my hands gripped into the sand.

I start running after you to grab you by the arms and shake you with rage. How could you talk to me like that? DON'T YOU REALIZE HOW MUCH I'VE DONE FOR YOU? But then I slow down as I look at your small frame, slender even for a seven-year-old, and watch your shoulders heave. You are crying. I walk for a while behind you. You glance briefly over your shoulder to make sure I am there, then you keep on moving, but slower, not to escape, just to move. Your head lifts and you start to look around. You lean over and pick up some seaweed and hold it up, like a flag, into the biting October breeze.

I think of your face yesterday, when we found a live crab on the beach, your hair blowing wildly as you jumped up and down with excitement, your hands working some imaginary device in front of you. "We could take him home and put him in the aquarium with Squirtle and I could take care of him and I could still have him when

I grow up and I become a marine biologist!" I explain to you that the crab is better off here, that the trip to Pelham will be dangerous for him, but we decide to transport him to the bay side of the island in a plastic bucket. It is a short walk. You give him seaweed for the journey and I carry the bucket. You talk to him, hunched over with your face next to the bucket, so that the crab can hear you and won't be scared. We lower the crab, now named Steve, gently into the bay and then you sit and watch as Steve sits motionless on the bottom in the sand. I say a prayer for Steve, who I am afraid has expired in our care, and hope that you don't notice. But you are optimistic.

"He's not dead, right Dad? He's just getting used to the new water." You lean your face so close to him that your nose is submerged.

"That's right, buddy. He's just taking it easy."

"He's going to live to be a hundred, right Dad?"

"At least," I say, as I pull you gently home. And who knows, maybe he will.

"Crabs live forever," you say with certainty, "just like moms and dads."

Why did we start screaming at each other? Because something you wanted to happen exactly the way you'd imagined didn't work out that way. You go crazy with frustration at an uncooperative world, and then I go crazy at you for being unhappy, when I try so hard to make the world perfect. If you can get so mad on a beautiful day at the beach, then surely I have failed somewhere. I rage at you for your lack of appreciation, but I am really raging at myself for my failure.

But now, as I walk behind you on a day that is all bright, whites and blues, I decide that it is not a gift to give you something then demand that you appreciate it. That demanded appreciation becomes payment required just the same as money. I give my children a gift when I give them something and let them take it or not, and do not require them to tell me what a wonderful parent I am. So I stride up next to you and I lay my hand on your shoulder and you tilt your head against my leg and say, tentatively, "Daddy, I'm sorry. Is something wrong?" As if nothing had happened. And I say, slowly, "No." I mean to add something serious, because I do not want you to get off too easily, but you smile your crooked smile and I laugh and say, "No, no, no." And then you let go of me and run ahead.

You dash straight into a group of gulls with your arms in the air, yelling. I almost shout, "Don't scare the birds," but what do they care? They soar up and over our heads, some swooping right back down at us. I cover my head with my arms and see you with your arms reached out, too. Except mine are up out of fear and yours are up to try and catch a bird. So we run through the gulls, with the birds whipping around and by us, as uncatchable as your dreams and my fears. You run straight for the deep blue crashing ocean. Now I do break into a run after you, to save you from the sea, like the heroic father I dream of being, every bit of my life propelled in your small black sneakers. ♥

Love

GREY HELD

On his night table, the Popsicle-stick project
we may never finish,
and on a shelf above, a boy
kicking the ball
on the Most Valuable Player trophy.

He adjusts his Little Magician's black pop-up top hat,
straightens one stuck finger of his white gloves.
He is so beautiful, it seems to stop my heart.
He picks up his white-tipped wand,
waves it over my head. *Poof!*

Lullaby

ELLIOT RICHMAN

Poised between man and boy, my son blasts
his trumpet to revive a dead hamster
on the family room floor,
in what is now his mother's house.

The man in him knows it is futile;
the boy in tears believes in Lazarus
and Santa Claus.

Balancing my checkbook, I listen
to the hope-instilled cacophony,
sounding more beatific
than all the choirs of the world
praising the deaf gods. 🐦

A Mother's Day Letter

∽ ANNE M. BRUNER ∽

Dear David,

I look at you, sprawled on the couch, your lanky frame in an extra-large Tazmanian Devil T-shirt and baggy, grass-stained jeans, your Steelers cap backward and your tennis shoes half-tied. I watch you, as you work your fingers like a keyboard, and know you're creating another video game inside your head. My son, at ten.

I remember when you were born. It was a sudden, fiery stab and it knocked the breath out of me. The force of it startled both of us. You really didn't want to be born; you liked the dark folds of womb. I pushed you with all my might. I was mad and, for once, you gave in right away. You burst out of me, as if you'd planned it all along and were just waiting until the last minute. Typical. You'll always do things in your own time, in your own way.

We both wept then, your dad and I, when we saw you, our son, alive. Even then, you were all gangly arms and legs spilling over the doctor's hands. How did you ever fit inside me? You must have wrapped yourself up tight and hard as the insides of a baseball.

I loved your little body. I loved your soft skin and tiny toenails and plump rear end. I was afraid of bathing you in the tub or sink alone, afraid I'd drop you. You were so wiggly! So your dad and I took you in the bathtub with us. Your floppy head would rest against my chest, warm in the grove of my belly. I loved the slippery-seal feel of you.

Our early days weren't all sentimental, motherly times, though. There were plenty of unmotherly ones. Dreary winter nights, I woke to your screaming, my nightgown pasted to my chest wet with milk. My arms ached from holding you. In the evenings, I snuck out to Drug Mart to get away from you. I roamed the aisles, dazed, and lingered over funny greeting cards. Then I dragged myself home to you, in your dad's arms, crying to be fed again.

Motherhood is a messy business. In the beginning, it's all bodiliness and it smells bad. Diarrhea and baby powder, mashed peas and wet flannel, all mixed together. For a while, those barnacle-like attachment days felt as if they would last forever. You surprised us with changes, though, before we expected them. You smiled and rolled over. You crawled, then walked. You began to talk. You laughed, arms wide open, as I lifted you from your crib in the morning. In a nasal, English-baby accent, you exclaimed, "A hoppy day!" Once, when I bent over to buckle your seat belt, you grabbed a straggly strand of my hair. "Bootiful!" you said.

Before I put you to bed, I often held you close and rocked you. Your favorite song was "Michael Row the Boat Ashore," and sometimes you joined in, humming a sleepy, "Ah, ah, you-la." As I lifted you gently over the rail, your eyes opened. You didn't cry out. Instead, you reached up to touch my face. I brushed your fingers with a kiss. "I love you, little guy," I said, every night. One night you replied, "Luf you, too." I closed the door and leaned against it for a moment, awash in a fierce tenderness I had never felt before.

I did not expect to go on like this. I thought I would reflect on Mother's Day and write a few memories from your childhood in a letter to you, but I got distracted by our beginnings. "So what's the point?" you ask. Now ten, almost eleven. Now love is too mushy, and you parcel out your kisses only occasionally. The point is that we are bound together. Call it Nature, call it Fate. (You grumble when I pull out that disciplinary line, "I'm your mother and you're stuck with me, like it or not!") Call it Love. Not love with strings attached, but love with ties. Love that gives, even as it crashes, bangs doors, and flings itself headlong into the future. Even as it will take off, let go, and say, "Good-bye."

Don't forget, that's all. That's my lecture, as you would say. I want to remember, too, every detail. We go round and come back, again and again. Each time, the circle widens. We embrace more. That's it. That's everything. Don't forget. I love you.

Mom 🐾

On Listening Again to "Stairway to Heaven"

STEPHEN CUSHMAN

thirty years after I lay down euphoric,
flat on the floor, head between speakers
the size of small coffins, I find myself

behind the wheel in the dark before dawn
driving my son to practice the drums
he's fallen in love with, his homework

assignment to study this song, blasting
as we barrel the interstate barely awake
under the stars, all mirrors quivering

with vibrating bass, until suddenly he says,
Listen to this, when drums without warning
break into a roll he cannot explain. I hear

the sound of him marveling and know when I do
my son can survive, as losses wreck less
in those who can marvel, and even though

we can't have much longer
than thirty years more, *listen to this:*
I wouldn't have it any other way,

since I wouldn't have him any other way. 🖤

Inspired by a Paper Route

∾ SUSAN LaSCALA ∾

My son is fourteen and needs money, he says, so he has acquired his first paying job, one that does not involve having his parents take out their wallets. I had to give the kid credit for starting a paper route in January, when New England's nights are fourteen hours long. Morning doesn't show its face until Will, in his dad's big Sorel boots, comes clomping back down the driveway with an empty bag slung over his shoulder. But he does it. He's up every morning at six, without any nagging. He gathers the pile of papers that have been dumped on the front porch, wraps an elastic band around each, and stuffs the lot of them into a canvas bag that bears a fluorescent orange shoulder strap.

One reward for Will is that the calico cat, Peaches, who does not reciprocate the boy's affection, seems to accept a truce at this early hour. She tucks her paws beneath her white chest and positions herself on a countertop to observe the sorting and wrapping. The newspaper preparations take place on the surface of the washing machine and dryer in our laundry room, which happens to be the same room in which the kitty's breakfast is served. She stays in dangerous proximity to the human she has otherwise designated as her enemy, with the hope that he might be sympathetic to her need for an early morsel.

For many years I have aspired to early rising, to walk or do yoga or start the laundry. Even better, I thought I might watch the nuthatches and chickadees shake out their feathers in the sun's first rays. But the flannel sheets have been too comfortable, my husband's body too warm to leave, and instead of getting up I wait to hear the second of the two alarms on the clock radio. I can only surmise that it is instinctive mothering that gets me out of bed now, an anxiety that simmers when I think of my son walking alone, outdoors, without a hint of light to befriend him. Never mind that I am five feet four inches tall, and that he has to bend almost in half to hug me. Whatever the reason, since the start of the paper route, I have had no difficulty hopping out of bed. At six o'clock. In the dark.

Sniffy the dog accompanies Will and me on these early morning deliveries. She and I usually have a daily walk anyway, but never quite so early. This winter it has been particularly challenging for the three of us to get to the neighborhood where Will must deliver the papers. We slither over an expanse of frozen lawn, then across the parking lot of the local boat ramp. On one morning, when we woke to find that a new blanket of snow had obliterated the boot prints from our previous walks, I strapped on my cross-country skis and followed Will over the unplowed streets. Later that day, a wave of sleet and freezing rain solidified the path carved by my skis. Now, weeks later, my lone set of tracks is still visible, frozen into the landscape even as the snows melt away from the edges. There are some days when we slip and slide and I fall, and wonder later in the day at my sore hip and neck and ribs until I remember—Ah, yes. The paper route.

The calendar has turned from January to February, and Will continues to be stoic and noncommittal about this job, in spite of the unrelenting cold, the footprints that melt and widen into Goliath-sized tracks that trip us in the crusty snow, and the fact that before tips, his salary is about ten dollars a week. But, there are rewards for both of us. A few days ago, on a morning that hinted that there might be an end to this winter, Will stopped in the middle of the road. He pointed to the sky. I stopped also, but appreciated something more than the orange and pink reflecting off a puff of clouds. After years of hearing myself say to this child (who would rather be punching the buttons of his Game Boy), "See the little dark-eyed juncos under the bird feeder?" or "Look at the silly trail that the crabs have traced across the sand!" or "There is a full moon tonight, come and see how it shines in the river," he, who had been unimpressed by my observations of the natural world, was pointing out the colors of a February sunrise . . . to me. 🖤

Snowflake

SUSAN TERRIS

Frost stencils windows.
In bed, boy on a sheepskin
burrows into darkness
as the mother kneels by his side.
Outside, boots creak snow,
and the sound of whistling
wraps night with bright ribbons
that ripple the air until
a dog-pack barks
and makes them fade.

I'll miss you, the mother says,
smelling sweet-hot boy-hair
and breath near her face.
Yes . . . the boy answers, as
his lashes butterfly her cheeks,
but I have our snowflakes.
Although she can't see them,
she knows they are there,
drifts of
odd, impossible colors

Next Steps

spanning walls and ceiling,
folded, folded, pinked with
shears into zigzag labyrinths
neither child nor mother
could have dreamed.
When I look at them,
the boy says, *even when
there's no whistling
and no dogs bark, I am
a snowflake and I can fly.* 🖤

My Heart's First Steps

A Winter Night

DAN SKLAR

I watch his back
as he turns on the light.
His pajamas have a pattern
of colorful biplanes.
I cannot see him
as he climbs the counter.
I hear him open
the box and pour the cereal
into a bowl.
I see him go to the refrigerator
and take out the water.
I hear him pour it in a glass.
I hear him crunching,
but I cannot see him.
I listen to it from
the dining room.
I can see the refrigerator
and hear its motor.
I see the white stove
and the back door,
the black outside.
The 1999 calendar on the wall.

It is January and it is bedtime.
He is eight.
I am forty-five
and can still feel
him in my arms.
This is sentimental,
but I don't care.
I hear him take a drink.
He puts the dishes
in the sink
turns off the light
and goes upstairs.
He does not see me
watching him, but
he knows I am there
in his confident night. ❦

Sick Child

∽ SUSAN HODARA ∾

It's always on the seventh day of a sickness that I begin to despair. It's then that it starts to feel like a permanent state, and a healthy routine seems doomed to unravel entirely. My heart sinks as I read the thermometer in my eleven-year-old daughter's mouth, climbing today to over 102. We've hit day seven, she and I, and every time the thermometer beeps, I feel frustration stewing in the pit of my stomach. I want her well and my will is utterly impotent.

The antibiotic prescribed by the pediatrician has been ineffective. What we first thought it was it obviously isn't, and whatever it is, it hasn't improved. Tomorrow we have another appointment, but my faith begins to weaken.

She lies now in my bed, on my husband's side, which is closer to the television. She has dark circles under her brown eyes. She's pulled the blanket up under her chin. She's cold, she tells me, her eyebrows arching upwards over her nose; she's chilled from the fever. Her shape under the blanket hardly takes up any space.

When she came home sick a week ago, it was almost exciting. Routine slipped away in favor of comfort and rest. I called the doctor. A part of me loved to have an excuse to just stop. I focused on edging out the sickness and for a few days, I felt competent and strong, and in spite of the sickness, happy.

But as we approach day seven, enough is enough. I'm not getting any work done, barely finding the chance to wash the dishes from one thrown-together meal to the next. And though I've visited the school daily to pick up assignments, I worry about what my daughter is missing. My heart aches because I see now that her plans for an after-school gathering, for a sleepover, for the sixth-grade social that she's been eagerly awaiting since school began, will fall apart. It breaks my heart as I watch her face crumple into tears when she realizes this, too.

The fever is getting worse, and now there's a cough that breaks the silence and keeps her from sleeping. She has no appetite and begrudgingly appeases me by eating a Ritz cracker with peanut butter. One. I look at her already-skinny schoolgirl legs and wonder to myself if they've gotten even thinner.

In the evening, she has a spell of feeling better. Aha! I think to myself, *You see, it's over now, just as you knew it would be.* I don't say anything, but offer her the thermometer, which showed her temperature had climbed again, just as it had before. My spirits plunge. My daughter can see the discouragement on my face.

"Come here," she says gently, and I let myself sit down beside her on the bed. Her arms are outstretched to me the way mine have been to her so many times, and I let myself rest my head on her shoulder. It is so small, this shoulder, not at all big enough to hold my head, but her arms wrap around me anyway, one hand patting gently near the top of my back. I can feel the heat of her fever rising from her skin.

"Don't worry," she tells me, her voice confident. "I'll be better soon." She says this while still patting my back, stroking my hair. My eyes fill with tears of exhaustion. We sit there and I let her soothe me, her words like a mother's, her voice still a child's.

As I write now, she's on the mend. The doctor diagnosed her sickness and prescribed medication that seemed to work within hours. Her body cooled and for the first time in a week I wasn't even curious what her temperature was. I heard her laugh with her sister, a sound I hadn't heard for days, and in a flash, my usual perspective returned. Routine, chores, work. Without giving me a moment, the demands of a healthy life announced themselves. It was hard to remember that just a few hours earlier, my sphere had narrowed to something as simple and frightening as health. ❦

A Book

GREY HELD

My older brother sent a Time-Life animal book
for both my sons to share—
my older brother, who never did read
any book I recommended.
Zachary is pointing to a photo of a tiger with his teeth
in the bloody flank of a zebra.
Jesse's big blissful head is resting on Zachary's
    shoulder
until the chapter ends and Zachary
slips a toothpick in to mark the page
and they must choose in whose room
to store the book. They argue over
ownership—brief, custodial, purely
a matter of perception, a matter of survival,
reprisals, outrage, a matter of flaunting words
they aren't supposed to say, like *hell, damn,*
stomping toes, yanking hair, pinching flesh,
careful to stifle each outcry, to only
fight in whispers, so I won't hear. ❦

The Bath

TARA MOGHADAM

The children are feuding again.
It happens in the bath.
It's the younger two butting ideologies.

The girl is insisting that God is everywhere
(and may even be a woman).

The boy barks: *Uh-ah! Are you trying to tell me
that God is*
*in this bathtub? Are you trying to tell me God is
in that toilet?*

He points at the cool ceramic seat near the tub.

The girl holds her stance. She is the older of
the two.

Don't you know God lives in the sky?
Don't you know anything?

The girl maintains her cool. She has seen it
before.
Every time she steps outside she *feels*
what God looks like.

Now the boy's face is red and fevered.

You can't tell me that God is in that toilet!
Uh-ah, Uh-ah! You can't tell me that!

He makes a big splash. Leaving
puddles on the tile, he mutters into his towel:

Women! 🖤

Goodnight

PAUL HOSTOVSKY

Out of the purpling blue
my ten-year-old son
lays down the law:
"No more kissing,
Dad.

There's my reputation.
There's Robby and Nick.
And Mark Agostini.
Think,

what would they think?"
His shame touches mine
as our eyes meet and glance—
his up to the ceiling,
mine to the floor.

We shake on it then.
No more kissing.
I nod, bow,
back out of his room
and turn out the light,

but leave the door open
exactly a little—
according to his
specifications.

Like hanging a picture,
we eyeball the angle
together. And I open
more. More.
A little
more. 🖤

A Plea for Kindness

∞ SUSAN HODARA ∞

My twelve-year-old daughter, Sofie, involuntarily flinches when I lean over to kiss her good-bye on her way to school this morning. She's angry because I hesitated when she mentioned again that "everyone" was wearing heels to school and her sneakers were getting old, and because she feels left out when "everyone" discusses the latest developments on a television show she hasn't seen yet. I go home feeling deflated and shed a tear in the shower.

I've heard it before, but feel it particularly poignantly this morning. Just as our daughters begin to blossom into womanhood, exuding sexuality and everything else that accompanies it, we their mothers have hit middle age. Though many of us have good reason to remain unintimidated—our bodies trim and strong from years of attention, our professional lives more productive than ever before, our minds vibrant and supported by the wisdom of our age and experience—it is nevertheless really happening.

I can tell not only by the lines and shadows that appear on my face when I get tired, by the sagging of flesh no matter how hard I fight, but also by the choices I make about how we spend our time. In our family, the television is never on during the week because by the time we've finished with homework, not to mention the regular succession of phone calls for both Sofie and her nine-year-old sister, Ariel, it's always later than it should be, and why is it only I who remembers how hard it was to wake up the morning before? I'm not one for phony phone calls or late-night sleepovers (at our house or theirs), and I continue to prepare broccoli and cauliflower even when it's usually me who eats most of it night after night. Simple, defensible values, but oh-so-vulnerable to attack from budding adolescents surrounded by a slew of peers who appear to have endless time to keep up with television shows, movies (R ratings included), and MTV; shop on a regular basis for new outfits; talk on the phone for half hours at a time; and still get all their homework done.

Yet we all have our flaws. We all miss out on something, fall short if not here, then most likely there. Too fat, too ugly, too soft-spoken, too flirtatious, too young, too fast, too snobby, too weird. Too boring, too strict, too overbearing, too annoying, too rigid, too conservative, too dense, too old. "Don't be so quick to judge," I tell Sofie. "Look to what's inside." But she's twelve, and I must admit, it took me many years beyond that to learn the value of an open mind. Complaining, judging, rejecting—particularly when it comes to one's immediate family—seem to go hand in hand with becoming a young adult.

I am facing it head-on with my twelve-year-old, who has always been generally sweet, reasonable, and good-hearted, but who seems to have developed an especially effective ability to roll her eyes. I'm having trouble taking it sitting down. "I don't deserve to get on your nerves," I tell her. And it's not just these almost-teens who can make life prickly. It's the woman who jostles you on a busy sidewalk and glares with a hatred summoned from somewhere entirely removed.

It's the waiter in a restaurant who answers with an edge of impatience when you ask just one more question. It's the boss or the teacher or the landlord or the cabdriver, anyone who speaks with rudeness or a lack of respect, who can leave you, if at all vulnerable, feeling small. Each unkind word, each casual criticism has the potential of developing a sharpness able to puncture the tires of someone else's self-esteem. The time lost now is irreplaceable, and even though it may be age appropriate, even healthy, for Sofie to be separating, rejecting, and redefining herself, I'm not ready yet for the pain that comes along with it. We are all hurtable, oppressable, and mine is a plea for kindness. ♥

Oath

PAUL HOSTOVSKY

For Pete's sake, I whisper
because it's the most benign oath I can muster
as I peel out of the driveway with my son
buckled up in the back,
having just picked him up at his mother's

whose oath was neither whispered nor benign,
but still hangs poisonously in the air outside the
    house
into which she's retreated,
the screen door slamming behind her.

Who's Pete? he asks,
snaking out of his seat belt to rest his little mug
in the place just behind my ear.
And what's Pete's ache?

Together we watch the road to my house unfold
like an old familiar story
while I tell him the story of Pete,
the guy who said he loved Jesus so much
he would die for him.
And that was his ache.

But when the time came,
when the soldiers all came
with their swords and their spears blazing
like the sun—
he got scared.

And he didn't do
what he said he would do.
And that was Pete's ache, too. 🌿

Making Pancakes

Carolyn Adams

Sunday mornings,
my mother cooked pancakes,
hot and fluffy
with syrup lingering at their edges.
My father worked in the garage
shaving yellow curls of pine
from new wood.
My parents kissed in the kitchen,
when breakfast was ready,
joked about trading in each other
on a newer model,
then deciding not to,
for they'd broken in this one so well.
The morning poured out
and they stood in the bright light,
hands clasped over hips,
smiling into each other's eyes.

Life was simple and golden then.
I was small and the rest of the world
was far away.

My Heart's First Steps

When I married,
he was not the keeping kind.
We kissed in the kitchen
in front of our children,
we joked about giving each other up.
And we did.

Now, Sundays,
I make breakfast while the sun shines,
and my children play.
I am the only one
they turn their small faces up to.
I mend their toys,
I make them wear coats,
I ask them to explain, and I listen,
and get tired of listening,
and try and give up and start over.

On Sunday mornings,
making pancakes is the best
I can do. 🐝

Next Steps

Second Birth

∽ P. M. HAYES ∾

Ⓦ Terry Tempest Williams once wrote of a mother elk that stood by
and watched as a grizzly bear devoured her calf. The grizzly sow's
cubs stood behind her. When the mother grizzly had filled her
stomach with the elk's calf, she tossed the remains back to her cubs.
When they, too, had had their fill of the carcass, she buried what was
left of the elk's calf and then laid on top of it for a later meal. All this
time the mother elk stood at some distance and watched, helpless to
save her offspring whose fate lay in the hands of something more
powerful than she.

She is only fifteen, my daughter, and though physically present,
she is gone for days at a time, enveloped by the impenetrable shield
of adolescence. I glimpse her now and then, see the old smile and
know that she is somewhere inside of this unrecognizable intruder.
I hear her laughter, hear her as she used to be, as she disappears out
the door and into the night.

I cannot keep my arms around her, cannot shield her from the
grizzlies. It is my turn to stand aside; I am the mother elk. I despair
over the brutal force with which we are separated during this period
of adolescence. I grieve the death of my mirror image as I am

dismembered, a piece of myself taken from me. This flesh of my flesh now slams doors in my face and refuses to speak. "You wouldn't understand," she yells from her bedroom refuge. My insides wretch and I am forced to ask myself, for whom do I grieve?

As she struggles to be born into adulthood, I must now return to my original role and give birth; it is time again to push her out into the world. But now it is different. The first time, she was born into my arms needing me, needing to be nurtured and protected. At this, her second birth, she is born out of my arms, seeking release. She shoves nurturing aside with annoyance and scoffs at protection. She relishes risk, rushing into the world at full speed.

It is with this second cutting of the umbilical cord that a river of blood and tears is released and I am caught in its current. It is a much more painful birth the second time around. Now, I have known her. Now, I have loved her.

I would trade. I would physically birth her again—it would be less painful than this emotional labor of disentangling our interwoven lives. I bleed this time from the words that become thorns and penetrate my skin as I desperately try to prune, rather than destroy, our intricate roots. And even as this work consumes my energy, I know it is for naught. As often as I get a glimpse of the old smile, I also get vehemence and anger, as if she will somehow be sucked back into the womb if she lets her guard down, if she admits even for an instant that we are still mother and child.

This job of parenthood offers no consistency. It demands that I flow with an ever-changing current. Just as I have become adept at providing a secure and nurturing environment, the peaceful waters of childhood have become the raging falls of adolescence. Needs and expectations changed overnight. It's time to brake, step aside, change course midstream, stop protecting, stop nurturing, step back and allow her to fall, pick herself up, and fall again. I stand in the shadows, watching her grow, wringing my hands to keep from reaching out. My own exclusion from her life is the one gift she asks for.

I am tossed and upended, treading water in unfamiliar territory. "Let go," is the order, cut her raft from mine, cut the cord that connects us, let her flow away from me and toward her own current. My heart struggles to cooperate with the command it's been given. I am able to make only small incisions in the cord, it frays and the knife slips from my hand over and over again. She picks it up and hacks at the connection. I watch, knowing that she is doing the right thing. I know that this second cutting of the cord is imperative for her. The broken cord if left intact would only wrap around her neck, deny her oxygen, and eventually strangle the life from her.

We are tossed abruptly backward, falling away from one another. The cord is severed. We stare at each other, seeing two lives now, where once there was one. ❧

A Blue Stone Turning

Stephen Frech

At night, I see a blue stone turning—
how easy to say it is the moon
or a blind man's eye that looks like a planet,
clouded, atmospheric,
when it is more likely my own eye wandering,
loose in its socket,
to find a favorite fish in the aquarium
and keep it a secret:
the fish that circled my dreams,
the fish I said I would marry,
the fish buried in the earth with each seed.
The fish is blue at the gills, indigo really,
and there are times I want to be
on the other side of that glass,
though I know it would kill me.

The blue stone in an earring
a young girl just had pierced
turns and she swabs it with alcohol every day.
The task is tedious, but she remembers,
does it more than is required.
In fact, she leaves the dinner table,

stands on her toes to see herself
in the bathroom mirror,
and she turns the blue stone.
She is a young girl and pretty,
sees only these beginnings
of growing into the beautiful woman
who is her mother.
She'll return to the table and tell no one
what she's done or what she hopes to be.

A blue stone is shown to me.
I say, *It is blue; it is a stone,*
and then cry myself to sleep for a week. ❦

The Truth I Carry

∾ ANNA VIADERO ∾

My boys, Jason and Dom, and I are hiking Northfield Mountain. Northfield Mountain is a fake mountain, built over a powerhouse, but it's the first woods the city girl inside me could trust when I moved to the country of western Massachusetts fifteen years ago. My sons both walked these trails in my belly and on their own. They caught every frog in the pond and counted long lines of red efts in migration, picking each one up a moment to stroke its fine soft stomach before letting it go on its way.

Today we are halfway up the mountain and have come across part of a new ropes course, a tire tied between two trees. There should be four ropes holding it, but a bottom rope is loose and now the whole thing is as steady as sand. Dom, ten years old but still my youngest, wants to try it and I automatically assume he's too small.

"The ropes are too wide," I say, as he jumps on. His arms and legs are muscled from a summer's worth of play. His torso is spread open like a kite. I'm confused, because I can't remember when he got big enough.

As Dom tries to move, his natural grace gives in to his need to hurry and his steps are stymied. Jason, his five-foot-seven, thirteen-year-old brother, calls out encouragement. "Left hand up, right foot out," he says, in a voice that's begun to deepen. Even my tone-deaf ears can hear the change. In the sunlight through the maples, I notice Jason's reshaping, the slow turns of his body, his arms now like eagle wings, so long when they're unfolded, and his waist is a world all its own. When my mother visited in August and we prepared to go out for dinner, Jason's dress clothes had somehow shrunk. His pants ended midshin, and gapped by five inches at his belly. His shirt's last button stopped a hand above the waist of the pants. While I stood trying to process it all, his father calmly opened his closet and dressed Jason in a man's shirt and khakis, larger socks, and shoes that fit perfectly.

Dom and Jason cross the ropes safely and wait. It's my turn now. I step onto the bottom rope and pull the top one close to my chest. Two boys too big and capable to be my babies are smiling and cheering me on from the end of the course. Though the ropes are firm under me I have never felt more off-balance.

It was a good thing I never thought too much about motherhood. How the two tiny ones that grew inside me might have to be pulled into this world through a hole in my belly. (They did.) How children could be such significant teachers. (They are.) How the predictable rhythm of our life after our first baby came might trick me into feeling like an expert. (It did.)

Even before he was named, Jason taught me to be confident. He sent bubbles into my belly at four months to say he was okay. The elbows and knees that repositioned like clockwork at eight months were another message. The basketball my uterus became that July was him, too. And even though he arrived surgically, shortly after midnight under a sky my husband said looked full of diamonds, this child was fine. Just as he'd been telling me he was for the past nine months. He was fine. A boy. Jason.

He was the one who followed the directions in the baby books. He cried when he needed me, hushed when I cradled him, breastfed like he'd been doing it all his life, and slept through the night at eleven pounds or six weeks, whichever came first.

Dom was different. He caught me off guard with his extraordinary needs, and put a wobble in my world that I had never felt before. Dom's first Christmas came in the midst of a year disrupted by his inordinate and unexpected needs that wore us all down. In those holiday photos, my husband and I wear dark blue circles under our eyes. In one photo, Dom is screaming in my arms. Jason turned to me, terrified, and asked softly, "When will Dom be leaving?"

Dom's awkward growing, that no baby or child-care book had mapped out, came into my world like a hurricane and disoriented me. It blew the "Mom" inside me far, far away. I watched it fly out the window those nights he cried without stopping. I watched it gust and tumble that string of months where he would stay with no one but me. I watched it crest the horizon and almost disappear the night Dom, at three, had trouble sleeping because he saw murdered men on his bedroom floor. "How did they get in the window?" he asked, as I opened my blanket on the floor next to his bed so he could see me. He lay in bed and hung his head over the edge to stare at me, until his eyelids gave up and closed. I barely felt "Mom" those nights, sleeping on the floor like a dog. Nights I went to bed sobbing about the life I'd left behind—my sewing, my writing. I pushed the needles and pens out of my life, let them fly into the wind. "For now," I thought hopefully, but knew I'd thrown away my lifeline. Giving up for now was right, I'd remind myself day after day, month after month. I didn't dream it would be years until I saw proof at Martin's Farm, when Dom just stepped away from me without a worry, to chase a pig around the barnyard, and then behind the main house, where he couldn't even see me. I felt it then, finally. A rope beneath my feet. Solid. Unwavering. Sometimes it's just time they need, I realized. The arrow-straight path that a book charts is to keep parents happy.

In the middle of the rope course is a tire. It marks the halfway point. I have made it here, exhausted and panting. My confidence has been left behind, like the focus items I brought to Jason's birth: photos, music, and lollipops. Somewhere into the tenth drug-induced hour of labor, I told my husband to take them home.

"I can't leave you," he said.

"Put them out in the hall," I begged, unable to look at all that certainty, when what I felt was so uncertain.

Venturing out on the final rope, I feel elephantine. I'm weighed down by the extra pounds that stay on my body, despite my attempts at winning back a figure I lost while I cared for everyone else but me. My boys are even more intent on helping me now, because I'm struggling. I feel hopeful, until they move under me.

"Get out of there! If I fall on you I could kill you!" I yell, motherly.

"We can catch you," they say, their arms woven into something softer than the pine-needled ground. I stop and let them help me, because they can. I inch out farther, until the safety of the tire is far behind me.

And then I am stuck. I tell my boys I can't move. They need to

My Heart's First Steps

help me get down. One pushes and one catches and we all fall in a heap on the bed of pine needles, the open sky a river of blue above us.

As my boys change and grow, I need to move forward in my mothering, too. To do that, I need to honor my time as a mother until now. Honor it all: the things I did right, the things I did wrong, the confidence that came with time. Life bumped me along the way, as life will, and never allowed me to erase, but only to color over and over again, making my own map. It's all there, and always will be, for me to interpret and reinterpret. I'll use it now to re-create the mother in me. Next time she tries on her dress clothes, they will be too small, cartoonish. I will laugh and I will cry and I will howl like a lonely dog. Then I'll move forward, no more the expert today than I was yesterday, but always the student. That's the only truth I'll carry. 🌿

Kiteflying

C. Pettit

A cupped hand releases
this painted lady
into the bell of evening.
It hangs, shaking, enlarged
like a moistened flower.
We learn its artless ways,
stumble in warm sand and
bite of salt.
Sea, wind pull and
shimmer in mirage
where over and over
we run together and play,
show each other through
fingers, wrists, precisely
when to hold on, make one
more launch into the endless
gold-streaked summer,
and when, catching the sweet
updraft,
to let it go. 🐚

My Heart's First Steps

Reading by Heart

∽ LOU MASSON ∽

Ⓠ Through the hall flowed the sound of my recently graduated daughter reading the latest adventures of Harry Potter to my wife. Her voice came to me slightly muted by intervening rooms, more melody than words and sentences. I knew the rising and falling notes well, knew them from years and years ago.

As a child this daughter would sing herself back to sleep if she awoke after we tucked her in. Sitting alone some nights, I would by chance hear her song as it floated gently and almost inaudibly down the wooden hill of stairs. And in those days if I imagined the song of angels that was the sound I thought I heard. Only once did I intrude close enough to hear the words: that night Christmas carols, or the parts of them she remembered, spliced in perfect harmony.

Throughout my daughter's life, we have had a succession of schnauzers who inevitably are by her side in family albums. And in one of the albums, or perhaps just in my memory, the three-year-old sits at the bottom of our porch stairs pretend-reading to one of those schnauzers, who snuggles next to her and eyes her knowingly. She told the story as she remembered my wife or me reading it to her. She read it by heart.

At bedtime I read to this daughter as I did to the older brother and sister who listened before her, and at some point she inveigled me to add short, made-up stories to the menu. Looking back, these may have been among the quietest and happiest minutes in my life; only further back in memory, snuggled in my own childhood bed listening to my mother or father in the near dark, do I find equal treasure.

A lifetime becomes a kind of library with each year adding a shelf of new acquisitions. And like other memories, the early ones imprint deeply and persist as intervening years confuse the record of middle age. One of the unexpected joys of parenthood may be reentering those old books in the company of a child whose pleasure and willingness to be carried away is infectious.

I think of those first listens and reads as nighttime activities, the story or rhymes a narrow bridge between the real world and an imaginative one, between wakefulness and dream. The stuff of reading, like a magic gift in a fairy tale, works a spell, slowly but inevitably opening our awareness and propelling us on to adulthood. It leads us out of ourselves. And yet its path is rarely straight, and in its crookedness it reveals not only what the literal-minded would call the real world but also the world of fantasy, make-believe, and imagination.

I do not recall when I began to read myself to sleep, nor when my wife and I let our children tuck themselves in. Perhaps it was like so many other passages that evade trauma or drama, paths that do not reveal themselves until they are well trod. Illness, nightmares, sorrow, and, once when I was a boy, a guilty conscience: only these could bring a parent back to the bedside, book in hand.

Accurately or not I link the reading-aloud habit with trips to the library. I well remember my first card, and my glee in first carting home the maximum number of library books. I think of the entitlement cards I've carried in my wallet: library card, driver's license, draft card, voting card, and credit cards. My worn library card may have carried me further and given me more than any of the others.

My daughter reads *Harry Potter* to my wife for the fun of it, relishing, I believe, the reversal of roles. My brothers and I read to my parents in their last days, the roles also reversed. I have no idea where our voices or the words we read took my parents. Did it take them back? Did they dream ahead to a better place without regret or pain? What was in their hearts? Unanswerable questions, perhaps. Asking someone to read to you seems very much like asking someone to remember you in their prayers.

I heard the poet William Stafford once say that he would give up all he had ever written to write something new, to go through the adventure one more time. This is as true of reading as it is of writing, for reading is a most civilized act—the one act of greed with high moral value. Often I have stretched out a good book anticipating the pleasure of one more chapter, or reread old favorites known by heart. These are pleasures I hope to enjoy for the rest of my life, the pleasures of traveling with good books between the waking world and whatever sleep befalls me. ❧

Alchemy

RICHARD M. BERLIN

I roll up my sleeves
to wash utensils she never cleans:
mixing bowl and measuring cups,
rolling pins and wooden spoons

covered with wet dough.
Years ago she began to stir
flour, sugar, water, and heat,
learned to beat egg whites

with a steel whisk, melt
chocolate on a double-boiler,
and we ate gold
cupcakes, shortbread,

begged for her coconut soufflé.
Up to my elbows in hot water,
I gaze out the kitchen window
at clouds rising in huge white loaves

over apple trees filled with fruit,
and I marvel that we made her
one green May morning
from our own sugar and sweat,

how we never imagined
this afternoon before her leaving,
a shoo-fly pie cooling on the table,
the smell of molasses filling the house. 🖤

Now Daughter

SONDRA ZEIDENSTEIN

Now daughter, when we sit across from each other,
necks thrust forward, talking about your work,
how you midwife babies into the world
and you skim with two fingers
your soft dry lips as you talk,
or trace a sensitive fingertip around your chin,
I remember how I stroked your cheek,
its fine red veins,
as you sucked the nipple of your bottle.
God! how long you would take sucking
with mild, half-interested puckers—
an hour almost for three ounces.
I think you had no appetite
for spending your days in my silences,
my other-mindedness,
when I wasn't fitting you into your pink nylon snowsuit,
tucking you deep in the shadow of the carriage,
putting you down in playpen, high chair, sandbox.
I think you wanted to hold me there,

My Heart's First Steps

make me look from the blue-and-white dance of
     television
to the small pink birth stains
fading between your eyebrows.
I wanted to sleep, to burrow into my darkness.
I gave you morning nap, afternoon nap, put you to
     sleep at six.
My dog—russet at the corner of my eye—
let my faint interest be enough, but you made me
watch your clear eyes doze up under your lids,
made me touch your cheek, tickle the small fat sole
of your foot, flick it with thumb and middle finger
until your body startled
and your lazy mouth remembered.
You set yourself against my darkness,
spun me like a thread from my knotted spirit.
You held me to the world. 🖤

Fathers Playing Catch with Daughters

∽ PAUL F. CUMMINS ∽

The award-winning American poet Donald Hall wrote a widely anthologized essay entitled, "Fathers Playing Catch with Sons." I'd like to add my own entry into the baseball conversation, which I call, "Fathers Playing Catch with Daughters."

In Hall's essay he says definitively, "Baseball is fathers and sons. . . . Baseball is fathers and sons playing catch, lazy and murderous, wild and controlled, the profound archaic song of birth, growth, age, and death." A beautiful sentence, but not altogether true. Baseball and softball are also fathers playing catch with their daughters; I have been doing it for twenty-five years. It binds us together, connects generations, and widens our appreciation of some of the old-fashioned virtues of America, just as much as it does for boys and fathers.

I married into two daughters. One was and is a harpist, so endangering her fingers didn't seem to be a good idea. The other enjoyed sports and, since I was a new guy in her mother's house, playing catch and shooting baskets were activities we could do together. Then my wife and I had two more daughters. When each girl turned two, we began playing catch in the driveway adjacent to our home. Soft underhand tosses at first, and then the next stage, when we both would throw overhand. We also tossed a small, then a larger football back and forth. The older, Anna, gradually developed great form and was good enough to be the starting catcher on her varsity high school team her senior year. If there had been a girl's football team, she would have been the quarterback.

Almost every day when I came home from work, one or the other, or both, would say, "Come on, Dad, let's play catch." It was our special time together. Gradually the younger, Emily, developed a cannon for an arm. After a while, I had to slip a sponge in my glove as her throws were stinging my hand. She was the Crossroads School's starting shortstop for four years and was twice all-C.I.F. She also played two years of Division I ball at Northwestern University. Even though both girls have now gone off into their own lives, whenever they come home, we play catch. It is still one of our bonds.

Looking back, I believe the games of catch were more than just a time of closeness; they were a toughening-up process, a physical lesson that teaches if you work at something, you can get better and better. Also, both girls developed a pride in *not* being precious wallflowers afraid to get their knees skinned or their hands dirty. They developed an openness to experiencing physical challenges. At first, a softball, and then later a hardball being tossed to them was scary, but they overcame their fears and progressed to longer and harder throws. Now, when they play catch together, or when Emily and her boyfriend, a former high school and college player, zip the ball back and forth, people stop to watch. Often the bystanders can't believe that a girl can catch and throw with such velocity and force, the pop of the gloves echoing across parks or streets.

I was never a very good baseball player; I didn't want the ball hit to me. And when my daughter Emily's team reached the C.I.F. finals for the first time and went into the last inning with two outs and a one-run lead (the winning run driven in by Emily), I, engaged in projection no doubt, was terrified that the ball would be hit to her. She, of course, wanted the chance, and when it was hit to her, she fielded it and calmly threw out the runner.

Yes, moments like that one were a source of pride, and now are delightful memories, but the lessons the girls learned were life lessons. Recently, the two of them traveled through South America with only backpacks. From Patagonia in Southern Chile through the rainforests of Bolivia to the top of Machu Picchu, often sleeping under the stars, they were not afraid. They looked forward to each new adventure as they had learned to look forward to each level of playing catch, from T-ball to Little League to varsity starting spots. A great deal began with a father playing catch with his daughters. ❦

Mowing the Lawn

❧ WARREN GARR ❧

As a very young child I remember my father cutting the grass with an old gas-powered reel-type mower. The running motor and the whirring blades, the smells of cut grass and gasoline entranced me.

Feeling the powerful vibrations of the engine through the handle was both exciting and, at the same time, frightening. Dad would let me put my hands on the rubber grips, and his strong hands would cover them to help guide the direction of the machine. He was so powerful and comforting, almost mythic in my mind.

Then we would be off. The mower pulled us along as we adjusted the throttle to keep it at a steady pace. Dad and I controlled the turns, as if we were dancing.

After a few passes we would stop to empty the basket. I enjoyed the cut grass, smelling so fresh and new. I liked getting my hands into the cool green slivers, lifting out a large mass, and putting them into a bag to be discarded later. Sometimes in the garage I would spy a bag and put my hands in. A few inches under the surface it would be warm, even hot to the touch. Feeling the latent power of the summer sun stored in those bags always filled me with a sense of mystery.

As I became older, I lost the poetry. Cutting the grass became a chore. At times, I had to mow the lawn rather than go places with my friends. It became a responsibility instead of something that gave pleasure. My father and I were at war during those years. He had his traditional ways of doing "The Cut." I had new ideas that didn't seem to interest him. My arguments of having better things to do also didn't seem to carry much weight. I thought my father rigid and insensitive. Eventually, I went away to college and abandoned the lawn to him.

Over the years since then, I've continued to cut grass. I have my own family now with three teenage sons and I've taught them how to mow a good lawn. Like me, they loved it as small children. But I can see the writing on the wall. Already I see the beginnings of the "Grass Wars," for they have their own ideas of how to mow, and friends and activities that don't always include me. But that's okay and as it should be; one day, the cycle will close for them as it has for me. Dad, I finally understand what you were trying to show me.

Cutting the grass was your metaphor for teaching me about becoming a man. Your lessons were about responsibility and the satisfaction of a job well done. These were things I was not eager to learn then. I was too unseasoned, too full of myself to appreciate what you were trying to do. I was unable to accept it from you, and for that, I'm sorry. I can now look back and separate the lessons from the teacher. Peace has finally come and I've completed the circle. For now when I cut, I can sit back on the mower and enjoy the breeze, the cool green grass, and bright blue skies. I remember summers past and simpler times. And sometimes I'm again a small child watching the blades, smelling the chlorophyll, and feeling at home in your guiding hands. 🌷

Reflections from the Wading Pool

Holding the World Like a Boy

∽ TOM GRONEBERG ∽

When my son was born, I began taking afternoon naps. And in the three years since his birth, I find that I am taking them ever more regularly. As he grows and finds that he does not want to sleep, when my wife is home to watch him, I take naps in his place.

I put a pillow over my most sensitive parts before nodding off, a lesson hard learned from the times that my son cannot help himself, from the times he loses himself in play and tackles me, coming in for a crash landing, startling me from sleep. Other times I wake to find him staring at me, waiting for me to get up, his hair golden and unruly over moon blue eyes. Sometimes he leaves me a present balanced on my chest, a token of his play. The tiny yellow monster truck, a dime, a plastic letter with a magnet embedded in it that he has taken from the refrigerator door. He leaves these toys, these pieces of his world, for me to wake up to.

My son has a way of holding onto things that I do not. Heading into the grocery store from the parking lot, I will absent-mindedly hand him the car keys. Then, after shopping, I forget that I gave the keys to him and I panic as I search my pockets in the parking lot, ready to call a lock-out service or head back into the store to scan the aisles. But he is holding them, looking at me, grinning, the light in his teeth. He has had every toddler opportunity to let the keys slip, fall down the storm drain, to trade them for something more fun. Yet he clenches them in his fist because I gave them to him.

He holds onto the world in the same way, does not want to let go. He fights sleep, does not want to go to bed at night or take a nap with me in the afternoon. He holds onto life tightly and does not care to be gone from the action in the time it takes to sleep. At night, he brings small toys to bed with him, wanting to have them to play with when he wakes up, not wanting to part with them. In the morning, they are still in his hands.

I wish I could hold onto the world as tightly as he does, but I always seem to be losing some part of it. My hair is fading, my hearing is going, my stomach spreading. The weeds are taking over the lawn and the gutters have never been cleaned. I have to remind myself that these things are not important; they are not anything to measure the world by. I have a beautiful wife, a wonderful son. This is what matters.

I know that I can give my son the small things that make the world run—car keys, house keys, a credit card, the checkbook—and that he will hold them. But I also know that I need to give him the big things. I need to give him the best of myself, every day, as much as I can part with and more. And I will remember that he will not misplace any of it. He will do more than safeguard these parts of me; he will give me pieces of his world in return, balanced—just so—over my heart. ❧

Heart Home

MARY CUMMINGS

1.

I was nine when sent to summer camp. My chest constricted, became alarmingly tight, hurt when I turned in my cot. The camp nurse declared: "You are *homesick*." Amazed to be sick for home, amazed that emotion could take up forceful residence.

2.

When I saw a plaque in my grandma's house telling me, "Home Is Where the Heart Is," I thought maybe I knew something about that, but couldn't say exactly what.

3.

Someone told me when I became a mother that my love for my daughter would be so beyond what I feel for my husband. She didn't know I love him like Elizabeth Barrett Browning declares, coos, sighs in sharp joy. Do other people compare love? I cannot measure him against her, her against him. Yet, there is this homesickness for my child: distress at our separateness of body and space.

4.

My baby's hand squeezes and wrings my heart like those charismatic healers who plunge a hand and pull out vitals without a knife. She's my heart walking around naked—valves, arteries pulsing and dancing in joyous pain. 🌱

Diapers and Deadlines

∾ ANN REILLY COLE ∾

I waited a long time to be a mother. Time enough to have first been a daughter and a sister. A student, an entrepreneur, a landlady, a homemaker, a financial manager, an investor, a wife. And a professional artist. These roles have not vanished in the ten months since my daughter's birth. The time available to do them, well that's another story.

Physically, the transition into motherhood was easy for me. Oh, yes, there was the pain of childbirth, the tiredness, the recovery from surgery, but pain subsides. Sooner or later, sleep cures tiredness, and it's amazing how much routine work can be done in a tired state. The hard part for me was dealing with the acceptance that, for now and the near future, I cannot be a full-time mom and the kind of artist I used to be. The artist had to change.

At first, I trained myself to focus quickly on my painting, working in the studio whenever I could manage. Sometimes I had just enough time to lay out my paints, only to find them dried and useless when I returned from the latest demand for my attention. And I hated spending my day wishing Taylor would just fall asleep so I could finish a project. I'd waited too long to be a mother not to savor the experience. I made a decision. No more deadlines. It's a pretty awful word to have as part of one's routine, anyway.

My artist's cargo van was traded in for a station wagon, a visible reminder that my professional life was diminishing. I felt a terrible loss. The shiny, new, family-friendly vehicle did not match my self-identity. Can I still be an artist, if most of the creative thoughts I have live only in my head? I've known many people who talk about being artists who haven't picked up the tools of the trade in years. Was this my fate?

There is no possession I would not sell or mortgage to provide for my daughter. Not the hand-carved monk's writing table that I bought on payments when I lived in Florence, Italy, or the pocket watch that my grandmother wore on her wedding day. These choices are easy. The hard choice, the scary choice, is setting aside my professional life. Other mothers have told me that it doesn't get easier to manage time until the children are grown. If this is true, I will be sixty-one years old when I rejoin the professional world. My marketability will have been severely compromised. How will I save for my retirement?

When my daughter was born, I wondered when I would feel different, feel like a mother. What does it feel like to be a mother, anyway? I was getting an idea that it was different than I imagined it would be. My mother was my definition of mother. She'd been a mother for nineteen years before I was born, so in my mind, *mother* was a finished thing. I asked my mom when she first felt it, and she said when she was alone with her baby for the first time. As soon as I was alone with Taylor, I paused to think about my feelings. Nothing different. I thought, well, when she calls me Mommy, that's when I'll feel it. But instead, I have come to a gradual awareness of being a mother. I don't remember the moment. I am becoming a mother all the time.

My belief that raising my daughter is the work God has placed before me guides me. My faith that God will provide for our needs helps me manage the anxieties and stresses that come with the decision to set aside my career. At times, I resent that my husband does not have to make this sacrifice. He still goes off to his teaching job. He has his salary and pension plan. He comes home and spends long hours doing remodeling projects, and enjoys the satisfaction of his accomplishments. I struggle to get a creative half hour in between cooking, cleaning, laundry and dishes, shopping, baby care. I have no weekends off. Then I remember. Many moms don't have a supportive partner in life, health insurance, or a living wage. My husband is a good father. He doesn't get to spend as much time as I do with our daughter, and he misses out on many adorable moments. I know, too, that it discourages him when despite his best efforts, he is unable to comfort her and she cries for me to hold her.

So I endeavor to be grateful for this time, and put my best self forward. It's not hard, not really. She is a happy, bright child. Her four-tooth smile is never far off. Our daily gigglefests are better than Prozac for keeping the blues away. Raising Taylor is exactly what I want to do now. It is interesting and monotonous and fun and frustrating and overwhelming and satisfying and wholly worthwhile. As I get to know this new little person, I get to know a new side of me, too. I'm learning more about my own ability to adapt and find creative solutions to life's problems. My new job as an artist is to find a way to bring my inspirations to life, within the boundaries of my lifestyle. My job as a human being is to be fully engaged in the work of mothering that is at hand, and to share it with others in a meaningful way. You know, it's kind of like making a piece of art. Only better. 🖤

My Heart's First Steps

Becoming

∽ PHYLLIS WALKER ∽

When contemplating what my life has come to and where it is going, I find myself questioning, looking back, questioning some more . . . what was the plan? When I was twenty, what mattered to me and what did I want the future to be? Have I reached my goals, accomplished my dreams? I wanted to make a difference in the world, to leave it a better place. These thoughts go through my mind as I rock my little son tonight.

It's late, the house is dark and I am holding him close. I listen for each breath, watch for signs of distress, and feel to see that his chest is rising and falling. He was born with a breathing problem called infant apnea. The walls of his air passages are so thin that they periodically collapse and his breathing stops. It is something I'm told will correct itself with time. There is nothing the doctors can do. There is nothing I can do to make him stronger. I have found that blowing in his face when he stops breathing makes him gasp, which reinflates the collapsed airways. It isn't that this process is difficult; it's that I am constantly in a state of alert, listening, watching, waiting.

It's been three months and I'm weary beyond belief, but I'll continue this vigil for as long as he needs me. He is my son and I gladly give. The fear of loss was constant at first, but as the months have passed, I've gone from fearing every moment to treasuring it. As I rock my son, I realize that my goals are being achieved right before my eyes. Not noticeably to anyone watching my life, but I can see it. What am I doing? I'm being a mother, changing the world with each of my children.

Whatever compassion my three older sons learn from watching me with their littlest brother as I struggle with his breathing, this is the measure of compassion they will turn and give to others.

When laughing and splashing come from the kitchen and I see our two-year-old skating on the tile floor, covered by a gallon of spilled milk, his little hands laughing and splashing all over the walls and cupboards, I have a choice to make, and I choose laughter over anger. Whatever tolerance I have for his sense of adventure will set the limits on his creative dreams. I want him to know that dreaming is the first step, trying the second, learning the third. He helps me clean up and we talk about the day we can go to an ice rink to skate.

When tears of exhaustion cloud my eyes and I wonder if I can go over multiplication tables yet again, and I think, "Does this really matter?" I realize that no, the multiplication tables won't change this child, but the patience he learns from me is something he will carry forward into his life forever.

My oldest son tells me of his dream of time travel, of the theories he's studying to see if it's possible. He believes in this vision with so much conviction, and I'm tempted to plant his feet firmly back on the ground, but my mother-heart rises up within me just in time and I remember to encourage him, to allow him to release his mind to new heights. Validating a child's dreams gives them the power and vision to try.

I struggle daily to become the person I should be, knowing I am only as good a parent as I am an individual. It is love for my sons that helps me find opportunities to give them the lasting gifts of patience, encouragement, joy, forgiveness. These gifts I give them they will hold inside, and in the dance of their lives, spinning, revolving, holding close and finally letting go, they will turn and give these same gifts to others, the world becoming a better place, one child at a time. 🌸

Renga of an At-Home Dad

~ BRADLEY EARLE HOGE ~

My three-year-old son wakes me in the morning quietly saying, "Daddy?" at the side of my bed. After a long day of defending the dog, cleaning Cheerios off the carpet, quieting their cries and playful screaming, giving them dinner and baths, I miss them once they are asleep. I cradle him close to me, waiting expectantly with eyes closed for the baby's waking cries across the monitor.

I wonder, with broom in hand, how much earth is moved by the sweeping of the kitchen floor? Dirt brought in by a three-year-old and his dog, swept into a trash can, carried to a landfill. Is it enough to level mountains, to build new ones where mountains never existed before?

I sit in the hot sun on a hard wrought-iron chair with my infant son in my lap while my three-year-old learns to swim. I am surrounded by mothers holding books and talking, while David squirms to be put down, struggles to hold the bottle himself, fusses because he is hot and past a nap. I hand him to the lady next to me, who asks to hold him. The mothers tell her how cute he is. I take my sons to appointments, restaurants, on errands, to museums and parks. The mothers smile, children stare, other men comment, "It must be nice to have the day off."

I watch a mound of gypsum grow like sand through an hourglass onto the parking lot from my son's shoes, having chased lizards across dunes at White Sands, New Mexico. How many shoe-fuls will it take to change the vector of migrating dunes? To defy wind and carry the abandoned lake to ever more arid landscapes: parking lot, van carpeting, washing machine run-off, car wash vacuum?

I have conversations in the car with my three-year-old sitting behind me. "Daddy, you be Superman, I be Batman, okay?"

"Okay," I say, leaning back to hold the bottle for the baby.

I play on the floor with my sons, the older one's cars, doctor kit, and train tracks, the younger one's rattles and balls. The dog brings his chew toy. I sigh, standing in front of the toilet, whenever I hear the pattering of little hands on the bathroom tile, the gleeful giggling of the baby as he crawls toward me, until I must stop what I am doing to pick him up and hold him as he watches. I sit at a restaurant table late at night, after everyone else's needs are met, with a cup of coffee, plenty of milk, and a piece of chocolate cheesecake. Taking care of myself after a long hard day with the one-year-old throwing food and tantrums, testing his limits, his favorite game. Poised with pen over open journal, trying to think of all his precious moments.

I watch my son build mountains in his sandbox, the same one I built in mine as a child. The actual self-same one, and the same as my father built. Mountains aren't eternal, after all.

I stand in a cadre of neighbors, conversations over beer and barbecue, while the children play within earshot and peripheral view. The men implore me not to dispel their myth: going to work must be harder than staying home with the kids.

I watch the quick replacement of sincere interest with confusion and discomfort every time the question, "So what do you do?" is answered honestly. Changing conversations to polite chitchat, since women are not sure how far to open up about shared experiences and concerns, and men no longer have any way to connect, no shop talk or masculine asides, no nods or winks to offer.

I rock my baby to sleep with a bottle while the three-year-old watches a movie. The dog sleeps in the chair he's not allowed to be in. I'll chase him out as soon as I put the baby down. I carry my sons to their beds at night, rituals of kisses and acquiring the right collection of blankets and stuffed animals. They talk to their menageries to fall asleep, and I cannot go to bed myself without leaning in to look at them.

I take a few hours off on Saturdays, sit in coffee shops or restaurants, to write poems and get a break from the kids, but I miss them as soon as I'm alone in the van. Power struggles, temper tantrums, ear infections, mud tracked into the kitchen, juice spilled, sibling rivalry, broken toys, ant bites, bumped heads, hurt feelings, night terrors. Riding bikes to the park, pushing swings, teaching, answering questions, holding a sleeping child while he's sick, sharing epiphanies and laughter.

I've come to understand, the best times as a parent are spent with your children at your worst moments: reading them a story with a sore throat, picking them up with an aching back, making them laugh when your patience is thin. 🌿

How Much Is a One-Way Ticket
to Somewhere Else?

∽ MAUREEN HELMS BLAKE ∽

I don't know how much more of this I can take. Two decades of being in a two-parent, one-income family—with fifteen of those years spent navigating the uncharted waters of homeschooling, all on a subpoverty income—have taken their toll on me. Why am I homeschooling? Why did I ever have children? Why did I even get married? I know I'm nearing overload when I find myself convinced of the allure of a room inhabited only by a bed and myself.

Remembering that I voluntarily chose these pathways offers little comfort. I find it hard to recapture my original motivation for making these decisions. Though I dig deeply into reserves of inspiration, ingenuity, and humor, too often I come up with clenched and empty fists. Convinced of my abiding love for my family, I admit to myself that the emotional shortness of breath and bouts of testiness are screaming at me to take a major step back and reassess my life, before greater harm is done.

During some semialone time, I drift back in thought. I remember that one of my happiest mothering experiences was breastfeeding my third child. After lasting only a week or so with my previous children, I was thrilled to become skilled at the art of nursing. I had no preconceived plan for when nursing would stop, only that as I considered breastfeeding to be a two-way relationship, I was content to continue until we were mutually ready to outgrow it.

Imagine my dismay when I woke one day with an aversion to being nursed. This physical attachment to my daughter seemed to symbolize all the ways people were plugged into me. Finally that afternoon I cried out, "Don't let her get near me!" I was sure that if she nursed one more time, I would be sucked inside out and disappear. I'm not ashamed to own up to it. I know that it was frustration speaking, using my voice.

My husband came up with some ways for me to have some small yet crucial freedoms. He slept with our daughter in the living room, took her for extra walks, rocked her when she wanted Mom. This got me past a few rough days until my equilibrium was restored. My daughter and I went on to have another year of nursing until the desire on her part faded and we both gently outgrew it.

All these memories come flooding back as I continue to sort through the confusion and discomfort I am currently feeling. The next step for me is to quiet my thoughts in prayer. I've always looked to God as my heavenly parent, and have prayed to know what was best for my family. I take time now to recall the decisions my husband and I have made: to have our children born at home, to nurture them through breastfeeding, to have at least one parent home with them, to homeschool. We didn't have any master plan. At each stage of development, my husband and I challenged ourselves not to go the traditional route unless it felt right for us. And often, it did not. The paths we found ourselves on were lightly traveled, full of the excitement of discovery yet forbidding in their strangeness. Taking time to prayerfully review my initial vision and sense of purpose reminds me why I am on these roads.

Another step is to share my frustrations. My husband knows many of them, but his current work involves overnight hours. He can't do much more than meet his own needs and obligations right now, so I find solace talking with a friend. At first I doubt she can truly empathize unless her life mirrors mine, but I am quickly comforted, despite the different paths of our lives. The sweet sympathy of two women caring their ways down parallel paths soothes me.

I also talk with my daughter, now thirteen. I have already shared with my children some explanation for my recent crabbiness, trying to explain my need for a little distance without sounding as though they are the problem. As I muse out loud about how to carve out some rejuvenating time and space, my daughter challenges me to be specific. Given our current house, finances, and responsibilities, what can I realistically do?

The answer that surfaces immediately is to find a place to be alone, if only for a few moments. Discounting the bathroom as a possibility, I think of the easy chair in the study. I'd have to close my eyes to be at peace there, since too many reminders of "things to do" would surround me, but a day or two of reorganizing just might turn it into an oasis. Then when a moment arrives, planned or otherwise, I'll be able to grab it.

A couple of weeks have passed since I first recognized the warning signals. All I've done differently has been to take time to listen to myself and remember the nursing experience. There, balance was regained after I stepped back from the draining demands of the moment, found ways to take a deep breath, and then continued on the journey, refreshed. And now, even though family life has been unusually busy, peace has been the undercurrent, not pandemonium. I don't yet have a success story about this season in my life. But I have gained a palpable peace from honoring my own voice—listening to and writing these thoughts. A crisis has been averted; some breathing space has been gained. What I do with it remains to be seen. ❦

I am tired . . .

CATHY LENTES

I am tired of motherhood.
I quit,
resign,
withdraw from the fray.
Children, go back to the womb,
to perfect possibility.
Let me dream
what if,
someday.

I am tired of homework,
pick-up,
clean-up,
taxi.
I've done diapers, toddlers,
term papers, last minute miracles
in blue macaroni,
clay maps of Ohio,
and soda volcanoes.

I am tired of heartache.
Two A.M. fevers,
cracked bones,
bloodied noses,
sleepless nights over grades,
junior high heartthrobs,
fragile friendships,
all the worst parts of high school
worried again.

One friend says I nurture too much,
let them go, let them
fend for themselves.
Pretend you have ten children, she says.
How would you handle it then?
I groan.

Motherhood is hard,
harder than algebra,
harder than pie crust,
or safe sex.
Somehow I qualified.
Me, still lost in the living
of one life, let alone five.

My Heart's First Steps

Yet, yesterday
my youngest said earnestly,
Mom, I'll still love you
when you're wrinkled,
and ugly, and gray-haired.
I'll even come see you.
I won't leave you.
So, I guess I'll have to stay.

But they'll go.
They began leaving when I hatched them,
when their father first
pulled me close in the night.
Even then, they were borrowed.
Teachers of patience, life
in the moment, all Buddha's
best lessons, creatures of shadow
and light. 🖤

Looking Beyond the Clutter

∽ AMY PINNELL ∾

⟨◊⟩ I spend many moments during my day surveying the demolition done by the little hands of my two children, ages five and two. Take the kitchen, for example. Within minutes, pots and pans and wooden spoons are spread wall to wall. Papers and magnets that were pulled from the refrigerator litter the floor. As I maneuver around, cereal crunches under my feet and I step in a puddle of apple juice, which soaks through my sock. Crayons fresh from the box are broken, stripped of their paper, and left under the kitchen table in seconds, and paper sacks are pulled from storage to become skates. Make no mistake, these kids are good at what they do.

I've come to the conclusion that children were born to make messes. I affectionately call it Creative Clutter. It's the nature of children to experiment with everything. Led only by their excitement, they jump from one activity to another, unhindered by what they leave behind, and there simply is not enough time in my day to pick up everything. I'd rather be on the floor with my kids instead, coloring with crayons or making paper hats, or flying them high on my feet playing airplanes.

This evening, with the children in bed, the quiet wrapped around me like an afghan, the rhythmic tick of a clock the only sound in the silence, I begin my walk among the ruins and feel a sudden fondness for the clutter of our lives. A purple ponytail holder, a flowered barrette, a tissue that wiped a runny nose. Dirty socks peek at me from under a chair cushion. I place the drawings of stick-people holding hands back under the magnets on the refrigerator. I pull a piece of orange candy out of the carpet, and empty the half-full milk glasses into the sink. I put the plastic people back in their plastic beds, and the books in their basket. I brush cheese crackers, scattered on the windowsill, into my hand, then throw them in the trash. I see the pie pan that was a swimming pool earlier in the day. A mound of dolls smile at me where they lay, drying on a towel, after their bath in the sink. I notice the purple flowers, one-inch-high weeds, given to me by my daughter. "Mommy, I picked these for you," she told me with a small smile, and I am flooded with the ordinary sweetness of my daily life, which is all around me. The poignancy of it grips me, and with a mother's heart, I must go one last time into my children's rooms, to kiss them good night. 🌿

Beauty in Bending

Lisa Rye

I used to be picky about trees tilting

until no one noticed my *perfect* Christmas tree.
For two months I glued ribbons and flowers,
(color-coordinated to suit the room, of course)
on Styrofoam balls,
sprayed plastic white doves gold,
assembled the tree balancing color and design.

Tada—
I threw a party—
Blah blah blah.

The next year, my husband surprised me
with a green fir dotted in white lights,
wrapped like a mummy in miles of white cord.
I escaped to the fabric store,
bought fiberfill to conceal the wires,
made it appear as though a snowstorm had passed
    through.
The kids said, "This is our prettiest tree yet."

What about the year I spent hours
making the perfect Christmas tree?

My Heart's First Steps

This year the boys took over decorations.
They admired their completed work
oblivious to the angled trunk.
"It's our best yet."
I cocked my head sideways to view their creation.

So trees can tilt all they want.

I read about an exhausted woman who
propped a ladder in her living room,
and hung balls from the rungs.

Now that's the spirit.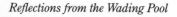

Humble Pie

∽ LESLIE J. WYATT ∾

In my parenting journey, I have eaten many helpings of humble pie. I must say I'm glad that it is not as fattening as chocolate cake. There have been so many things that I vowed I would or would not do with my kids. So many "Nevers. . . ."

"No child of mine is going to have a runny nose that goes unattended." At twenty-three, I thought it the epitome of neglect to see a child's upper lip slick as a glazed doughnut. With the supreme arrogance of ignorance, I could think of no reason why any parent who *cared* would have a child with a dirty nose. Enter child number one. And two. And so on, up to six. I have, in the past seventeen years, endured many a glazed-doughnut nose, and must confess that I now have a much better understanding of how difficult it is to keep up with the little rascals, to say nothing of enduring the pitiful wails and sore little noses. Before two years of parenthood were up, I heard myself saying (around a forkful of humble pie), "I'm waiting to wipe her nose until it reaches her lip."

Baths. I hadn't realized how far from my original mark I had fallen until I was leaving some instructions for my husband. "Don't worry about baths, just make sure they play in the wading pool periodically, and wash their hair on Saturday night." I've found that a smile is a good sauce to have with humble pie.

Bedtimes. As newlyweds, my husband and I discussed at length and in beautiful rosy colors how our children-to-be would toddle off to bed at our first request, and how their sweet little voices would not be heard again until the next morning. I guess nobody had told us that other people's babies would sleep through the night, but not ours, or that drinks, kisses, hugs, stories, potty runs, and tucking-ins happen more than once per child, per night, or that often, the older ones start a heart-to-heart conversation when you go in to say a final good night. So much for those "just the two of us" evenings.

If I had written them down, my list of "Nevers" would have been endless. But somewhere in the process, I realized a very important truth—never say never. Instead, as my children have grown, a list of "Alwayses" has emerged.

Always let your children know that you are blessed to be their parent, and that you consider your job as mom or dad to be the most important and most rewarding in the world.

Always seek to bed them down in peace, with the assurance of your love, all ruffled feelings resolved, and greet them every morning with the same love.

Always keep in mind that someday, these children will be grown. Dirty fingerprints on the woodwork, coats on the floor, spilled milk, and a zillion and one things to attend to aren't forever. Nor are little voices saying funny words, little hands around your neck, little giggles in the dark. 🌸

Where Have All the Bears Gone?

∽ DEX WESTRUM ∾

I didn't become a father until I was fifty-three years old. Having been out of the loop all my life, I had no idea that the bear was the totem animal of newborn boys. By the time my son Clayton was twenty days old, he had received at least fifty bears. Not only did they arrive as stuffed toys ranging in height from a few inches to a couple of feet, the bears also came on T-shirts, blankets, daytime clothes, sleepers, flower pots, and numerous greeting cards.

I am a little uneasy with these bears. They are all of the soft, cuddly variety. Like Clayton, they are cute and wide-eyed. But unlike my son, the bears are not ready for life. Human encroachment into the wilderness seems to have driven bears—real bears—farther and farther from our daily lives. Consequently, real bears are further from our imaginations. These soft cuddly bears, designed to comfort evolving infants, are deficient in bear-ness.

We are a long way from the days of the plains Indians who insisted that young men should not only hunt bears, but also should eat of their raw, steaming hearts. A young man who had eaten from the heart of a grizzly had made the bear's fierceness a part of himself.

To be able to say, "I have the heart of a grizzly inside me," was a pivotal rite of passage.

While not exactly fierce, Clayton is full of bear-ness. He loves to howl and growl and snort at the air, especially when he is waking up. I like to think that he is announcing the arrival of a new bear in the woods. The other day when I was changing him, he came off his back and attacked one of the stuffed bears we had placed along the edge of the changing table. Clayton took the bear's nose in his mouth and slammed it from side to side, giving it a good thrashing.

Clayton's mother thinks his tendency to howl and growl and snort at the air is the result of her diet, from eating foods that have never agreed with her. But I know better. The soft, cuddly bear is not a fit totem for a young man whose first impulse is to subdue stuffed animals. Even though Clayton has only managed to bite off the nose of a soft and wimpy bear, he has the heart of a grizzly. 🐾

Mommy's Inner Animal

∾ ALICE KEANE PUTMAN ∾

I walked down the driveway of our quiet, suburban home, my baby in the stroller and my three-year-old next to me, on our way to the playlot. The street was deserted, as usual. Most of the people on our street work outside the home.

It was a cool, gray autumn day. A large, white, windowless van was driving slowly down the street. It wasn't unusual in any way; it could have belonged to any plumber or carpenter, but some instinct told me to take my baby out of the stroller and hold her. The van pulled up, stopping in front of our driveway. A man in the passenger seat rolled down his window and smiled politely. "Excuse me," he yelled, shaking out a map. "We're lost."

I couldn't say what made me apprehensive, but I knew I wanted myself and my children as far from the man and the van as possible. "No," I said. "I don't want to talk to you." As I backed away, he opened the van and stepped out. I had the keys to our minivan, parked behind me, in my pocket. Without thinking, I turned, opened the door, put the baby down, and lifted my three-year-old into the driver's seat. As I straightened, I could feel the man standing directly behind me. I knew that if I tried to get into the car with the kids, he would grab me.

I pressed the lock button on the door and whispered to my daughter, "Honk the horn and don't open the door for anyone but me." The man reached from behind, trying to grab the keys from me. I froze, stunned.

Then, with a sudden fury, I backed into the man, digging into his stomach with my elbow. I caught him off guard, and as he fell, I kicked him between the legs. He screamed and began to scuttle backward like a crab, then turned, got on his feet, and ran to the van. He and his accomplice raced away. Suddenly, I was very tired. I let my clenched fists fall to my sides and leaned against the minivan. I looked in the window and saw my daughter honking the horn. She looked back at me, and smiled. "The Bad Mans were scared of you, Mommy!" she said proudly. "Yes, they were," I said.

These are my daydreams since my children have come into my life and in them, we always make the Bad Mans go away. I'd thought that becoming a mother would make me gentler and sweeter, would soften me. And toward some (my family and close friends), that has happened. But since having children, I no longer feel unable to defend myself. I know I can do it. The stakes have been raised. I would gladly place myself between my family and the harm that could come to them and amazingly, I know there's something in me that would put fear into the heart of even the most dangerous criminal. I call it the Protector, and I think that every woman has one.

I imagine it sitting quietly in the lower reaches of my brain stem, waiting to be awakened from its near-constant slumber by a combination of my adrenal gland and intuition, particularly when my intuition tells me that someone is dangerous to my children. And it has taught my conscious mind not to seek out excuses for other people's behavior, if they are too curious or too interested in me and my family. It has led me to snarl at a man who grabbed the handle of a grocery cart that my child was sitting in. It has led me to tell people, with no polite overtones, to go away. It has moved me away from the nice-girl politeness I was taught as a child, and has led me to teach my daughters that being nice can be overrated, and to listen to the voice of their own inner animal. And every month or so, when I have one of my vivid daydreams about what I would do if the unthinkable happened, I am grateful for it. ♥

Career Girl, Interrupted

∾ SARAH BARNES ∾

⟨👋⟩ There's this stack of clothes in the middle of the hallway that I keep stepping over. It's a potential pile for Goodwill. I walk by it several times a day, but I'm having a hard time taking that final step of putting it in the car. Topping the pile is a Banana Republic suit, along with some chunky black shoes from my fashion-conscious, career-girl self of the mid-1990s. Under it is the grunge ensemble I used to wear to clubs when I was trying to look like I was in my twenties. Then a tangle of various belts that have lost their way. It's not so much these clothes that I'm letting go, but the old Sarah, skirt by skirt.

I think about the time in my life when I wore these clothes. I was sure I had the coolest career in the world as entertainment editor for a newspaper in Austin, Texas. I liked nothing better than being among the first to hear from the critics about the newest play in town or a local band that just got signed. At thirty-three, I was leading meetings and making important decisions about how to cover a city known nationally for its music scene. I was on the ladder tackling my climb, rung by rung. I couldn't wait to get to the paper every day to work that job, wearing those clothes.

I still remember the last time I wore the Banana Republic suit. It was a day where I wouldn't be discussing the latest band or Austin's growing opera audience. I'd be quitting a job I loved for a child I loved more. My husband and I had just learned that our daughter Meredith was developmentally delayed. We decided that helping her walk and talk would have to take precedence over my journalism career for a while. I knew we were lucky that I could make this decision, but, like so many women, I didn't leave that office for the last time without lots of uncertainty and a bit of sadness.

My life over the past three years has been about playgroups and doctors' appointments and therapy to help my daughter Meredith reach her milestones. Right or wrong, I have approached it like a career. My day is no longer about editing, fashion, and music. I spend my hours helping my daughter catch up. We've used a hat with a chin strap to keep her jaw from jutting. We put patches on her eyes to keep them from crossing. We put braces on her legs to ready them for walking.

Today she is four. If I had a job review for motherhood, I might be put on probation because the goals I set for my daughter's progress have been elusive. She's not walking on her own yet. She has no real words. We're told her vision is never going to be perfect and there are no glasses to fix that.

I no longer look in the mirror and see the career girl in the perfect size-four beige suit. I see a mother who wears faded Levis nearly everyday and tries to part her hair so that the least amount of gray is showing. I see a journalist that never found answers to why her daughter's brain developed differently. But I also can see a woman who has found a more gentle side of herself. I still go to meetings except for now they are at my daughter's school and I tend to listen more with my heart. I don't get to be the first to hear about new art exhibits coming to town anymore, but I savor every awkwardly drawn picture Meredith brings home because it's proof she can hold a crayon. And, my instincts tell me she's going to walk and she's going to say, "Mommy," even if I have no papers telling me that.

There will come a day when Meredith won't need me so much. I hope when that happens, she won't put me in the hall for Goodwill. 🌸

Animal Dreams

Dane Cervine

If I were a baboon, my son could hang from my body
as I went about my day, and this he would do
gladly, nuzzled into fur, ear pressed
to the sound of a single heart
beating within us both.

If I were a wolf, my daughter could follow
my soft padding feet along the rocky cliffs
deep into the forest dark, muzzle wet with scent,
smelling the things of this world a man could only name,
not take into his body as we do now,
this ripe dusk sweeter than any word.

As we are human, I gather my son and daughter
in midflight into hungry arms at the end
of day, twirl them like birds cascading
as wings into the empty space in my chest
where I have missed them oh too long—
the father, alone in the office
dreaming of baboons
and wolf cubs

this ache deeper than human
in the animal heart within. 🌿

Another Guilt Trip

∾ Darcy Lipp-Acord ∾

It isn't that Halloween ranks as high as birthdays or Christmas on my personal scale of importance, but being away from home when my girls, ages one and two, are old enough to enjoy it breaks my heart. And suffocates me with guilt. I missed Laura's first rollover, Carmen's first wave. And now this. Here is another milestone I will miss because of work. Here is another of their memories—will they remember?—which won't include Mommy. I'm missing their first trick-or-treating. I finish dressing the girls and swallow my tears. *It's three days in New York City,* I tell myself. *You should be thrilled.* But the Halloween costumes laid out on the couch bring up another sob.

The conference will help me organize an international youth cultural exchange, one of my responsibilities as a new Spanish teacher at our high school. When my boss told me about it, my heart leapt at the thought of spending three days in New York City. Until I realized I would miss Halloween. I then wanted to decline the trip, but since the school district had already paid for my tickets, I felt obligated to go.

My husband, Shawn, and I buckle the girls into carseats and drive the just-lightened streets to their new daycare. Grace, the owner, meets us at the door, smiling.

"They haven't had breakfast yet, Grace," I begin, but she interrupts, saying, "Don't worry, I'm always doing breakfast for somebody." Carmen is resting her head on Grace's shoulder. Grace hugs her and says, "Boy, we're going to have such fun! We're going to play games and do projects and try on costumes. . . ."

"Oh!" Another stab of guilt. "I didn't know," I explain. "I didn't bring their costumes."

"Don't worry," Grace says, "I've made costumes for Halloween for as long as I can remember. We'll just pull out the costume box and see what we find."

I hug Laura tightly, kissing her ear and whispering, "I love you." Grace holds Carmen out for me to kiss and her pudgy hands clutch at me as she tries to climb into my arms. Seeing this, Laura wraps her arms around my thigh and cries, "Mommy! I don't want you to go."

"Come now, let's go have some cereal!" Grace says brightly, disentangling me from their little hands. As I turn and climb into the truck, I hear her asking, "Cheerios or Froot Loops?"

Shawn rubs my left shoulder as we drive out of town, letting me cry. I'm obsessed with morbid thoughts of plane crashes. Will my girls be okay if I die? Of course, Shawn will love them and care for them, but will they be alright? Or will they be plagued with anger at a mother who left them for a silly conference and never came back? I try to pray. *Lord, just let them be okay. Let me come back. Please, I want to come back.* But prayers don't come easily. I'm still too angry at God.

I remember another time when work came before mothering. My swollen breasts told me I was pregnant. On a drizzly April morning, I took a home pregnancy test, then got out my dog-eared pregnancy guide and announced to Shawn that the baby would be

My Heart's First Steps

born at Christmas. But the next day was Monday, with classes to teach plus meals to cook and two toddlers to care for. Days slipped by, turning into weeks. Several times I started to call for a prenatal appointment, only to be waylaid by a child or a student.

In May, my breasts quit aching. Shawn asked when I would go to the doctor, but by that time, I was applying for a new job, planning our move to another state, and making arrangements to attend summer classes for graduate credit.

In June, on the second day of summer school, I lost the baby.

I will never know if our third child died because of my neglect. People tried to reassure me after the miscarriage, saying, "God took the baby for a reason," or, "There must have been something wrong." Maybe they were right. Or maybe my own actions were to blame. Maybe the baby died because I was too wrapped up in advancing my career to care for him or her. At the very least, I know that if I had taken the same care with that pregnancy as I had with my first two, I would feel less accountable for the death. We rarely talk about the lost baby these days.

As Shawn drives me to the airport, he tries his best to convince me that everything will be okay. He lists the trips he wants us to take with the kids. I smile and nod, all the while wondering if I'll make it home.

Inside the plane, I watch out the window as we climb higher into the blue, and I make a promise to myself. Someday, I won't miss Halloweens, special days, or ordinary days. Someday, I won't be too busy to care for the lives growing around me and inside me. Someday, I'll simply be a mommy, and someday I'll do it well.

Someday. 💚

Nights after Daycare

TONY REEVY

Trapped, as I often am, downstairs
in kitchen, laundry, bathroom.

Listening to tumbling feet
on bare floorboards.

Running—I can see it—up and
down with a scrap of paper.

A soft wish to be upstairs,
with the baby, rises.

Oh, the long road between
unpacking dirty diapers,

washing sour bottles, and
an hour spent with her.

Snow Days

∾ SUSAN EVANS ∾

It snowed four consecutive Mondays one February, which is unusual weather in Atlanta, a city of many hills and no sand trucks. First we lost heat and power; then we lost my husband, a hardy Detroit boy who scoffed at the idea of snow days and slid down the driveway to work.

I'd like to say I built a roaring fire and roasted marshmallows for cocoa. I'd like to say I pulled my son and daughter, then five and seven, into a lap filled with Golden Books and fuzzy bears. I'd like to say we all snoozed in a pile drowsy with warmth and shared affection. I'd like a second chance to make it so.

I built the fire all right. I had to, or the pipes would freeze. But I gave the kids chocolate milk, not cocoa, and I let them read to themselves by the fire, while I used our only flashlight to work on a report. Dressed in ski clothes, we napped in separate rooms to keep us from driving each other crazy.

My children are grown now. Do they remember those four Mondays, and wish they'd been different? Do they wish they'd had a mother who could play Thumper and Duck Duck Goose and make a snow day magic? Do they know that when I hugged them so tight they couldn't breathe and asked, *How could I live without you?* I was wondering how I could live with them, as well?

In my premotherhood days, I vowed I would make my children breakfast every day, drive them to school instead of sending them on the bus. I would eat dinner with my kids, even if it meant eating while the sun was out and dining on macaroni and cheese. I would attend every soccer match and each baseball game. I would be the central figure in my children's lives. When they remembered their childhoods, they would remember me.

I'm sure they do, but I'm also sure they remember me distracted and short-tempered. I finished my writing assignments at soccer practice, wrote acceptance letters to Montessori during the championship game of Northside T-ball. We ate dinner together every night, but sometimes I was so tired that I barely spoke. I skipped paragraphs in their bedtime stories, until the kids caught me. I rarely felt guilty then. I was too busy. But now?

Now I feel sad. If I'm going to live eighty years, as the actuarial tables say, my mothering days were a mere quarter of my existence. Surely I didn't have to be in such a hurry. But, who am I kidding? I was and I would be again. My daughter will be, too. She'll have different distractions, but she'll struggle with how to be a good mother and her own person, just as I did. She'll learn that unconditional love is a given, but unconditional attention is impossible. She'll vow to be the best mother ever, and wonder why she can't watch *Sesame Street* without a book. If she asks my advice, I won't tell her much. Each new mother has to find her own way. I'll just wait for a snow day, and when I think she's at the end of her rope, I'll call to suggest s'mores. It's not quite a second chance, but it's close. ❧

Grown Children

L. N. ALLEN

You know them as well as you know yourself
and not at all. It's as though the familiar
has entered the realm of Jules Verne,
where polliwogs turn into dolphins.

Like the mild shock
from storms that raise hair on your arms
but leave house roofs intact, parenthood is
at worst, not unpleasant.

Who is that stranger but your alter ego
only stronger, younger, and oh, so self-confident.
If this is pride and pride's a sin
you're both in deep water.

The problem is not to sink or swim
but how to suspend disbelief
at the walking, air-breathing proof
that somewhere along the line

between *give it ups, should've beens*
and *getting through the nights,*
you must've done at least one thing
incredibly right. ❧

Reflections from the Wading Pool

Reflections on Parenthood

∾ PAMELA MALONE ∾

It's like my garden. Great expectations not always met. Full of surprises, some good, some bad, and the main thing—no control over how it turns out.

I was absolutely delighted when I discovered I was going to have a baby. A total surprise, unplanned, there he was. To me, motherhood was a great thing, my true career, and I threw myself into it. I approached it scholastically and read books on natural childbirth, books on nursing, books on babies.

It all seemed so simple, and in a way it was, in the beginning. I worried about the baby, but there were always things I could do. It was like the garden. You plant all the neat rows and put the seeds in. You stake the tomato plants. It all looks perfect. You water and then you wait. And you don't think about woodchucks, or drought, too much rain or blight, tomato caterpillars, and just plain luck.

I remember at the time I was pregnant, an older colleague of my husband's said to us, "Just wait until they're teenagers. Then you'll see. And there's nothing you can do, it's downhill all the way!" Judgmentally, I figured whatever problems he had with his kids were his fault. In my naiveté, I thought there was a right way to parent.

And I, of course, would follow the right way. If anything, being a parent is a humbling experience. There is so much that we don't know, and we won't know, until our kids are grown. Maybe some of us never know it. They have personalities of their own. And sometimes when they suffer or struggle, our attempts to help backfire.

I'm the mother of two grown sons who are both intelligent, talented, good people. I love them very much. I had trouble letting them go. And out there in the world, one of them is now struggling like a plant without water. There is nothing I can do. The wild winds came, and he must pick himself up and do what he can to survive. I'm no longer his gardener.

He does not care that I devoted myself to the job, which I ranked as number one in my life. Sometimes, the baby grows up and screams at you, and gives you a low grade for the job you thought you did so well. There was no fertilizer! You left the hose on too long! You did nothing about the weeds!

At a certain point, you just have to let go. After all, my main intention was to do better than my mother, and didn't I at least do that? Maybe I was too . . . or maybe I didn't . . . maybe, maybe, maybe. But then, we learn that there are always maybes.

So what is a parent to do? Pray and wait, and let the nurturing skills go to the grandchildren. Because it's easy to be a grandparent. Yes, that's the answer. I have a new and wonderfully fulfilling identity as Grandma. And this job is a cinch. At least compared to being a mother! ❧

Not Polonius, But Your Father, I

JEFF CANNON

I realize I'm merely a caretaker.
You are only so much mine and so much more the
    song of that spirit
that dances in your eyes, pulses with your skipping
    rhythm,
bursts with excitement praising the epiphany of
    awesome wonder.

So I send you forth,
but not without some change in your pocket,
decent shoes on your feet,
an umbrella that I know you won't use except when
    I visit,
and a little extra stuff in your luggage I didn't know
    I gave you,
so open it carefully, there might be a spider or two
    deep down inside.

My Heart's First Steps

I meant well when I answered your questions with a
    story—
when I left you to choose and accept the
    consequences,
when I told you I still loved you and helped find
    Band-Aids for your soul,
when I cried about my limits to protect you from the
    softballs in your face,
the daggers in your heart and all the kicks and slams
    you would have to combat.

Remember what I told you when you were old
    enough to understand,
keep your wits about you and a keen eye on those
    you meet,
never take the "this" too seriously because the
    "that" will sneak up on you,
if you choose to feed a snake, be careful,
don't yell at it when it bites, for it will only laugh at
    you and say
"Didn't you know I am a snake?"

Don't lose your soul in trivia.
What you do counts less than who you really are
      throughout the days that mark your life. Don't
      let compassion slip through your fingers while
      grasping at some obsession,
beware the charms that suck your blood and leave
      your spirit dried up in the gutter.
Honor the dark along with the light and you'll
      always find
the middle way along your path.

How wonderful to watch you grow through the
      seasons,
and with each pruning blossom, double with some
      new-found gift
(Don't forget to write me after you call to speak with
      your mother).

Yes, I yelled and got upset, cursed and swore more
      often than intended.
So your father could be a fool as easily as the greatest
      guy on earth—

Yes, I pushed you to your limits testing sometimes
      with too harsh an edge,
only to toughen you up so I would know you could
      make spaghetti.
So maybe you wouldn't get hurt as much as me.

Remember all the hugs and kisses and my songs as
        you went off to bed,
all the rides in the car with stop-offs for treats.
Riding bikes and hearing you singing in the choir,
being companions when I drove around searching for
        a job—
despite the grief, life's an adventure.
You have the ticket in your hand.

In the midst of your mother's illness, when an
        anxious cloud hung about your young eyes,
I told you I believed in you.

Go forth now with my blessing.
Know that deep within your womb you carry all
        those sharp and soft pieces of me
along with the memories of ancient grandmothers,
the dreams of starry nights rocking in their cradles.

I wish I could take off with you to see and touch
        and feel
all that will be for you,
but that is for you.

I must stay here on the shores of the land that is mine
to nurture whatever tiny nuggets of promise remain.
Don't worry about me, I'll be just fine.
I will wait in the place where we will finally meet,
eager to hear all about your story. ♥

Reflections from the Wading Pool

Meet the Moms

Carolyn Adams has two children, now teenagers, whom she raised as a single parent after her divorce. In between raising her kids and happily remarrying, she has written more than eighty published poems. Currently, she coedits the poetry journal *Curbside Review*.

L. N. Allen is the mother of two grown children, born seven and a half years apart. She says, "When my daughter married, I returned to the poetry I had abandoned thirty-odd years before, when I met my husband—also a poet—with whom I didn't want to compete. I was wrong to give it up then, at least for that reason. But returning to poetry and learning a new craft in late middle age has been a blessing."

Rebecca Balcarcel holds an M.F.A. from Bennington College, where she received the Jane Kenyon Scholarship. She is the mother of three—twin five-year-olds and a seven-year-old, all boys. "I write in the middle of the night!" she says.

Sarah Barnes is a freelance writer living in Austin, Texas, with her husband, Jim, and daughters Meredith, four, and Caroline, six months. She says, "As the mother of one child with disabilities and one child who is developing typically, I see the beauty of both worlds in the daily miracles of two very different daughters."

T. W. Berry says, "I married my children's stepfather when my sons were ten and almost seven and my daughter was four, although now, eighteen years later, referring to them as 'mine' rather than 'ours' is inaccurate—as they and their trust in him grew, they gradually became his, too." She and her husband run a resort on a small lake in northern Michigan. Her poem, "Grand," is dedicated to MacKenzie.

Maureen Helms Blake has been a wife since 1974, a mother since 1976, and a homeschooler from 1982 until 2001, when she joined her three children at college. She says, "I am firmly convinced that parenting is a sacred calling and deserves a great deal more respect than our society currently affords it." She loves writing, simple cooking, acting, and being by water (even dishwater).

Robin Bradford wrote poems after the birth of her son because she had so little time. She is the recipient of a Dobie Paisano Fellowship, a Texas Literature Grant, and an 0. Henry Prize. Her monthly column, "Motherload," appears on *www.austinmama.com*. Robin lives in Austin, Texas, with her husband, their five-year-old son, two cats, and a dog.

Anne M. Bruner is a former high school English teacher and campus minister who now coordinates volunteer programs and edits the newsletter for Visiting Association Hospice. She and her husband, Michael Reiling, and son, David, live in Cleveland, Ohio.

Sarah Werthan Buttenwieser is the mother of three sons, Ezekiel, Lucien, and Remiel. Her fiction and essays have appeared in many literary magazines and journals.

Ann Reilly Cole was born a twin, the sixth of eight children in Elizabeth, New Jersey. A lifelong artist, exhibitions of her work began with a collage hung on her bedroom door and have continued with numerous shows in galleries in Europe and the United States. Now a full-time mother, she lives in San Diego with her husband and their daughter.

Mary Cummings is the mother of a young daughter. She is a poet, children's writer, and the Education Director at the Loft literary center in Minneapolis, Minnesota.

Susan Evans is the mother of four grown children—two biological, two step. She is a facilitator of bereaved parents, a trustee of Suffield Academy (a Connecticut boarding school), and has published a book about her experiences the year following the death of her oldest child. She practices hatha yoga, is an avid hiker, and is looking forward to her next parenting role as grandparent.

Joyce M. Fischer is a poet and a dancer. She lives in Verona, Italy, with her husband and two children, Zoe and Luca.

Marcia Gerhardt is a native Texan now living in Houston, where she and her husband raised two sons, Adam and Jason. "I tell everyone who will listen that boys are delightful and simple. I do not refer to intelligence, but to their innate ability to be themselves, at all times. They are the delight of my life and I am lucky to be their mother."

Jennifer Graf Groneberg lives with her husband of ten years, their three young sons, and a border collie whose primary occupation is herding the family's two doleful cats. As the editor of *My Heart's First Steps,* she invites you to visit the book's Web site at *www.myhearts firststeps.com*.

P. M. Hayes received her M.F.A. degree from Goddard College. She has published various essays on the subjects of motherhood, single parenting, and divorce. She facilitates a monthly writer's workshop and is currently working on her first novel. Pat lives in Freeport, Maine, with two teenaged sons. Her daughter is now nineteen and attending college in New York.

Susan Hodara lives with her husband and two teenage daughters, Sofie and Ariel, in Westchester County, New York. She serves as consulting editor for *Westchester Parent,* and was editor-in-chief of its sister publication, *Big Apple Parent,* where she received a Best Editorial award from Parenting Publications of America for her monthly column.

Karen Howland says, "I finished my master's in creative writing the week I conceived my daughter and have been ferociously creating our lives ever since, including the addition of a boy. My work as a mother has been such a fertile force for my writing, sprung from an inner well of intuition and women's wisdom that I believe is communicated from our ancestors in our very DNA."

Liza Hyatt is a printmaker, a mosaic maker, and a poet. She says, "When I am not home making messes with my daughter, I work as an art therapist. In this work I have watched many people reclaim whole, creative, spiritual lives."

Lysa James is the mother of two sons, ages nineteen and fifteen. "I found my soul mate when my sons were ten and seven, and together we have created a strong and loving blended family. I have pursued my dreams, however impractical the world might find them, and tried to teach my sons to do the same. Poetry put me on the path I was meant to be on and as a result made me a better mother."

Helene Barker Kiser is a stay-at-home mother and has been since the birth of her first child eight years ago. She says, "I wouldn't trade one day of this time, although the writing comes even more slowly than it used to. And that's saying a lot, since I have always been very slow!"

Susan LaScala is a nurse practitioner who lives in Gill, Massachusetts. She is often inspired to write about the happenings on Barton Cove, a little out-pouching of the Connecticut River, where she resides with her husband, two children, two cats, and Sniffy, the family dog.

Cathy Lentes lives on a farm in Southeast Ohio, near the Ohio River, with her husband and three children. Her writing has appeared in various journals and she is the recipient of numerous awards and residencies.

Darcy Lipp-Acord lives with her husband, Shawn, and their five children on a ranch near Ucross, Wyoming. Prior to deciding to stay home with her children, Darcy taught English and Spanish at public schools in Montana and Wyoming. Darcy and Shawn breed and raise registered quarter horses.

Pamela Malone is the mother of two grown sons, Joe and Otis. She always considered being a mother the most important job she's ever had, though she's a writer, editor, and teacher. She met her husband, Joe, at the University of California in Berkeley, but her children grew up in Leonia, New Jersey, where they return often for R&R as well as Mom's home cooking, which includes guacamole and pumpkin pie.

Anne McCrady is an East Texas poet and storyteller whose days are divided between performance, writing, gardening, and encouraging young people. Her poetry has appeared in literary magazines and anthologies, and has received numerous awards.

Tara Moghadam lives on the Puget Sound with her three children. She has been steadily shedding the skin of some past ambitions while reviving others. As an islander, she devotes her time to poetry, children, screenwriting, and yoga. In summer, she can frequently be found with her hands in the dirt.

Malaina Neumann is the mother of a daughter and a son, Isis Geneviene Divine and Llyr James Ra, and the proprietress of an online clothing boutique (*www.karmaboutique.com*). She lives in rural Virginia.

C. Pettit, with her husband Chris, raised their daughter, Sian, and their son, Dylan, in Milwaukee, Wisconsin, and Bozeman, Montana, where she currently teaches Spanish at Montana State University. Of parenthood, she says, "I find a sense of humor is essential and I need to remind myself that ultimately, my children do not belong to me, but to themselves." Her poem, "Kiteflying," is dedicated to Sian.

Amy Pinnell is a preschool teacher, writer, and mother of two. She lives with her husband and children in Winnsboro, Texas.

Alice Keane Putman grew up in Chicago, Illinois, and now lives in Vienna, Virginia, with her three children and wonderful husband. She is a lawyer who uses her legal skills to negotiate with her toddlers, and is currently working on an L.L.M. in tax law at Georgetown University Law Center.

Lisa Rye is an artist with a fine arts degree from the University of Michigan, and also a wife and mother of two sons. She writes and paints full time, and is currently working toward an M.F.A. from Vermont College.

Candy Shue lives in San Francisco, where she juggles writing and her family. Luckily, her husband and two daughters enjoy being juggled.

Susan Terris has been married to her husband David for forty-two years. They are the parents of three children, three in-law children, and twelve grandchildren. "I spend a lot of time with the grandchildren, and consider my role as 'enrichment' instead of 'baby-sitting.' I teach them to make things with their hands (my husband calls me 'The Project Woman') and I take them to live performances and art exhibits." She is the author of five poetry books and twenty-one books for children and young adults.

M. S. Tupper is a poet and mother residing in Maine. She thanks the following publications for inspiring and informing her mothering in valuable ways: the parenting books of Aletha Solter, *Mothering* magazine, and La Leche League's *New Beginnings*.

Anna Viadero writes easily and freely about family and mothering because it feels like something she was meant to do. Her writing has appeared in journals, anthologies, and has been read on public radio. She is the mother of two sons, Jason and Dominic. She lives with her husband and children in Massachusetts.

Phyllis Walker is the mother of four healthy, growing boys, and a new-born daughter. She lives with her husband and children in the beautiful Flathead Valley of northwest Montana, where she teaches piano and writes children's books.

Leslie J. Wyatt and her husband, Dave, have six children (Emily, 17; Allison, 14; Joseph, 12; Nathan, 7; Paul, 4; and Abigail, 3). They have a "sort of" farm in the middle/western part of Missouri, with chickens, a dog, a garden, cats, and more than their fair share of mice.

Sondra Zeidenstein is a poet, editor, and publisher living in Goshen, Connecticut. She has two grown children, Laura and Peter, and from each of them a grandson. Her children, born in Brooklyn, New York, were raised in the Bronx, Manhattan, Nepal, and Bangladesh.

Meet the Dads

Richard M. Berlin works as a psychiatrist in private practice and as an Associate Professor of Psychiatry at University of Massachusetts Medical School. His wife, Susanne, is a child and adolescent psychiatrist. Their daughter Rachel, nineteen, attends Williams College. Richard's poetry appears in his monthly column in the *Psychiatric Times* and has been published in a broad array of medical and literary journals.

Jeff Cannon is a former church worker turned social worker and poet. Jeff is a widower and father of two wonderful girls. "I work each day to pass on some teaching and to listen, hold, and rock rather than fix everything." Jeff lives in Vernon, Connecticut.

Dane Cervine serves as the Chief of Children's Mental Health for the county of Santa Cruz, California. "I love being a father." Dane lives in Santa Cruz with his wife and two children.

Roger Cody has worked in the United States and abroad in data communications, and he is active as a writer and photographer. Roger is currently studying Chinese brush painting at the Museum of Fine Arts, Boston, MA. He resides in Boston with his family.

Paul F. Cummins is currently president and a cofounder of New Roads School in Santa Monica, California, and the executive director of the New

Visions Foundation. Paul has, with his wife Mary Ann, four daughters, who are the light of his life.

Stephen Cushman is a professor of American literature at the University of Virginia. He is the author of two collections of poetry and three nonfiction books. Stephen lives in Charlottesville, Virginia.

Dennis Donoghue lives with his wife, Carla, and their three daughters in a 160-year-old Colonial on two acres with the family's two dogs, a horse, and a goat. Dennis teaches sixth grade in a public school. "As for my thoughts on fatherhood, it's the most satisfying endeavor I've ever engaged in, and maddeningly unrelenting at the same time."

Terrence Dunn is a lawyer in New York City. "I write on the train and after everyone else is asleep. I happily spend my free time playing kickball, drawing pictures, and doing anything else my kids want to do." Terrence lives in a small town just north of the city, with his wife, Elizabeth, and their two children.

Stephen Frech's daughter, Annalyse, is eleven years old. "Tenderness and patience became animate for me when she was born, and I worry, perhaps as many grateful fathers, that I have gained far more from having her in my life than I have to give. Our lives find us both inventing ways to bridge the miles between us, among them reading to each other over the phone when we are away."

Pete Fromm is the author of eight books, including the Pacific Northwest Booksellers Association Award winners *How All This Started*, *Dry Rain,* and *Indian Creek Chronicles.* His next novel is set in his home-town of Great Falls, Montana, where he lives with his wife and two sons.

Warren Garr says of his essay, "I wanted to show how a man can be brought full circle through interaction with his sons. There's nothing like the experience of 'walking a mile in someone's shoes' to give a father new perspective on what his father was trying to accomplish." Warren lives in Howell, Michigan.

Tom Groneberg is a ranch hand, a member of the volunteer fire department, and the author of *The Secret Life of Cowboys*. He lives with his wife and sons in northwest Montana.

Charles Grosel is a freelance editor, writer, poet, and stay-at-home dad. "Staying home feels right for me, as if I was born to it. That isn't to say I have the slightest idea what I'm doing. It's a seat-of-the-pants operation, for sure, a team effort, but I'd like to think we haven't gone too far off track. We'll have to ask our children in twenty years." Charles lives in Scottsdale, Arizona, with wife Betsy, son Mac, and newborn baby, Ella.

Grey Held's poetry has appeared in numerous literary journals. He says, "Being a father as I am of two boys, now ages twelve and fifteen, my emotions have run the gamut from pure joy to despair." Grey lives in Newtonville, Massachusetts.

Bradley Earle Hoge is an at-home dad for two boys and their baby sister. Many of his poems about fatherhood have been published in anthologies, as well as a number of small press magazines. Brad is "Dr. Brad the Science Dad" for his youngest son's preschool program. He lives with his family in Spring, Texas.

John Holbrook is the father of two grown children. "Fatherhood is still focused on unconditional love and physical affection. I could not be the father I am, however, without my wife, Judith, who always seems to have in reserve enough warmth, devotion, and patience to make the difference." John lives and writes in Missoula, Montana. His most recent book of poems is *Loose Wool, River Tackle, Pencil Drafts*.

Paul Hostovsky is a divorced father with a son, age thirteen, and a daughter, age eleven, who live with him half time and with their mother half time. "I live in the next town over, so it's just five minutes back and forth, which makes all the difference, especially when you forgot your soccer cleats at Dad's, or your math homework at Mom's, or half of your science project is growing in each of their refrigerators."

Clark Karoses lives in northern Idaho with his wonderful daughter, Maggie, and her devoted mother, Eileen. "My family provides a great deal of inspiration and support for my writing and I love them dearly. Fatherhood allows me to see the world through new eyes in a way I never could have conceived."

Peter Krok is the Humanities/Poetry Director of the Manayunk Art Center in Philadelphia and the editor of the *Schuylkill Valley Journal.* He lives in Havertown, Pennsylvania.

James P. Lenfestey is the retired award-winning editorial writer for the *Minneapolis Star-Tribune,* as well as the author of an essay collection and a play. He lives in Minneapolis, Minnesota.

Lou Masson has taught literature and writing at the University of Portland for many years, as well as being a contributing editor to a regional magazine. He lives in Portland, Oregon.

Todd W. Palmer teaches English to high school seniors. "I cherish my role as a father and can't imagine what I did with all of my time before my daughters were born." Todd lives in Port Orange, Florida, with his wife and their three daughters, Bailey, Ragan, and Savanna.

Guy Reed and his wife live in upstate New York with their two young daughters, where his wife works as an artist and stay-at-home mother, and Guy works at a greeting card publishing house. He has been a featured performance poet at several Hudson Valley venues.

Tony Reevy is an associate director of the Carolina Environmental Program at the University of North Carolina at Chapel Hill. He resides in

Durham, North Carolina, with his wife, Caroline Weaver, and daughter, Lindley.

John Repp lives in Erie, Pennsylvania, with his wife, the potter Katherine Knupp, and their son, Dylan, who continues to teach his father about heaven and hell and everything in between.

Elliot Richman is currently teaching college-level English courses on U.S. Navy warships. "*Lullaby* was taken from life. It all happened as described when my son was seven or eight, except that I've never balanced a checkbook. I was trying to use 'checkbook' as . . . well, the reader can figure that one out."

Dan Sklar teaches writing at Endicott College. "One of the joys of fatherhood is watching Max, who is ten, read to Sam, who is five. I love how they make jokes about my poems and interrupt me while I'm writing—it puts everything into perspective, they come first. Besides, there is nothing better to write about than them." Dan lives in Hamilton, Massachusetts, with his wife, Denise, and sons.

Paul Vos Benkowski and his wife have three sons. "I have been a stay-at-home papa for four years now. I will sleep when I die." Paul lives in Luck, Wisconsin

Norman Wasserman, a resident of Brooklyn Heights, is a veteran grandfather. His daughter Jennifer, mother of twin boys, later gave birth to twin girls, who came into the world the same way as their brothers.

Dex Westrum became a father for the first time just short of turning fifty-four. He is a stay-at-home dad who is generally exhausted most of the time. He is the author of *Thomas McGuane* and *Elegy for a Golf Pro*.

Acknowledgments

Thanks first to the contributors, whose writing forms the muscle and bone of this book; thank you, also, to the parents who shared stories that were not included here—your writing has become part of the book's spirit. My gratitude to Christine Engel and Judith Weber for early help and enthusiasm, and to Linda Hasselstrom, Nancy Curtis, and Gaydell Collier for inspiration and wise counsel. Everyone should have a kindred spirit and I am blessed with two—Laurie Buehler and Sara Esgate, who feed me books and kind words at exactly the right moments. My thanks to Claire Gerus and the staff at Adams Media for all their work on this book's behalf; special thanks to Courtney Nolan for her clarity of vision, encouragement, and careful editing. To my parents—Chris Graf, Fred and Pam Graf, Don and Joyce Groneberg, and my grandmother, June Oliver Vincent—many, many thanks. To my friends in motherhood, thank you. To Laura Nolan, my heartfelt appreciation for a lifetime of laughter and support. And I am grateful to my husband and sons most of all—without you, there would be no words.